D1529840

BERING SEA STRONG

HOW I FOUND SOLID GROUND ON OPEN OCEAN

LAURA HARTEMA

Skyhorse Publishing

Skyhorse Publishing books may be purchased in bulk at special discounts for sales promotion, corporate gifts, fund-raising, or educational purposes. Special editions can also be created to specifications. For details, contact the Special Sales Department, Skyhorse Publishing, 307 West 36th Street, 11th Floor, New York, NY 10018 or info@skyhorsepublishing.com.

Skyhorse® and Skyhorse Publishing® are registered trademarks of Skyhorse Publishing, Inc.®, a Delaware corporation.

Visit our website at www.skyhorsepublishing.com.

10 9 8 7 6 5 4 3 2 1

Library of Congress Cataloging-in-Publication Data is available on file.

Cover design by Mona Lin
Cover photo credit: Greg Westhoff and iStockphoto

Print ISBN: 978-1-5107-3151-6
Ebook ISBN: 978-1-5107-3152-3

Printed in the United States of America

Dedicated to those whose circumstances have pushed them to find their own strength and a better life.

"A ship in harbor is safe, but that is not what ships are built for."
—John A. Shedd

AUTHOR'S NOTE

My life has been shaped by all the people and experiences I've encountered along my path, especially those within these pages. Though individuals in this book may remember events differently, this story reflects my recollection of events and conversations, much of which were directly transcribed from my personal journals. The name of the ship and some, but not all, of the characters' names have been changed to protect individual privacy and anonymity. I hope my journey will encourage you in your own.

RUSSIA

INTERNATIONAL DATE LINE

Bering Sea

St. Paul Island

PRIBILOF
ISLANDS

ALEUTIAN ISLANDS

Amchitka
Island

Unimak
Pass

Dutch
Harbor

Unalaska
Island

SEATTLE
1,949 miles

Map created by Wendy Gable Collins

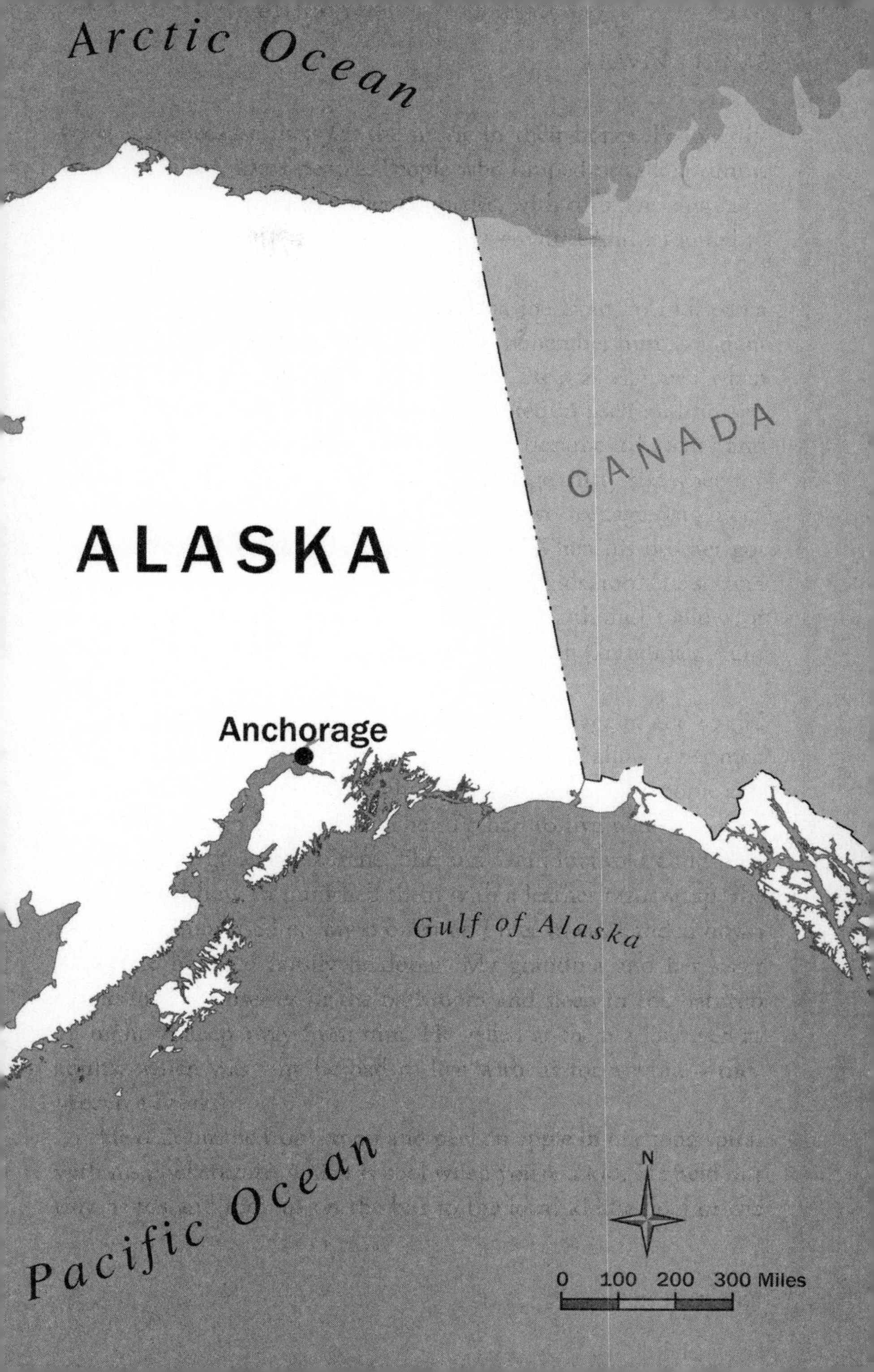
Arctic Ocean
CANADA
ALASKA
Anchorage
Gulf of Alaska
Pacific Ocean
N
0 100 200 300 Miles

CONTENTS

PROLOGUE

I stood bracing myself at the open hatch of our 141-foot commercial fishing vessel, only steps from a roiling sea and the incoming longline with pointed hooks whirring past my limbs. I knew why I was here. I thought about my path all the time. At age twenty-four, I fled the chaos of family, still tugging at me from the Midwest, to pursue my dreams of graduate school and an environmental career in Seattle. How could I have predicted that dead-end waitress jobs, disappointment, and rejection would push me even farther . . . to Alaska's Bering Sea, some of the most dangerous waters in the world?

As a fisheries observer, I would monitor fishing activities, sample the catch, and report the data back to the National Marine Fisheries Service (NMFS), where it's used to support sustainable fisheries management and establish fish quotas.

Ostensibly, I would also have to learn how to live and work side by side with these rough-and-tumble fishermen with no reprieve, a life for which no instruction manual or training video could have fully prepared me.

What's it like to spend three months as the sole female, an outsider, working among twenty-five fishermen aboard ship on the unpredictable Bering Sea, halfway between Alaska's remote

Aleutian Islands and Russia? In a time before cell phones, email, and TV's *Deadliest Catch* craze, I found myself there—on treacherous waters, in a frigid processing factory, beside a captain in the bare warmth of a wheelhouse, in a dark bunk of a shared stateroom, in cramped quarters, never far from the center of the dogpile. Many before me have sought Alaska, a land of back-breaking work and mind-blowing scenery, in search of escape, adventure, opportunity, and high wages. Some, like me, came from a life shaken and unhinged, but somewhere at sea, we discovered a strength we didn't know we possessed, strength we'd carry with us for a lifetime.

1

~~~

BOARDING

"ALL rows board immediately," the attendant said over the loud-speaker, as if we were under emergency evacuation. Whoever heard of a plane leaving early? My new friend and fellow observer, Stephanie, and I, having arrived minutes earlier from Seattle, funneled through the gate in Anchorage, only vaguely aware of the risks ahead of us. *I can't believe I'm doing this*, is the thought that keeps running through my head.

Over the loudspeaker I hear, "Inclement weather is fast approaching at your destination in Dutch Harbor, Alaska." Which is code for: "Board now, because the longer we wait, the higher the risk of going down."

With thirty-degree temperatures and snow mounting outside the airport windows, I shivered, despite the warmth inside the airport. But it would be worse up *there*; everything would be worse. I needed more time to think, to reconsider my impulse decision to work a ninety-day contract as a federally certified scientist aboard commercial fishing boats on the deadly Bering Sea. To the crew, I'd be a "fish cop," a "narc," a "snitch" of sorts, but all I wanted to do was accurately report what I saw and not stir up any trouble. Still, maybe they wouldn't want me there. The newspapers, media, and three weeks of training had forewarned me of the dangers, but the $2,400-a-month paycheck outweighed the risks. I'd have to work at my two restaurant jobs for three months to earn the same salary I'd make in one month at sea.

The other option: remain in Seattle as is—rejected from the University of Washington (UW) graduate program in fisheries and waiting tables to pay the bills. Seattle was booming with jobs for dot-commers in the 1990s, but there were few available for a twenty-four-year-old biology major. I wondered if I should forego my silly dreams altogether and crawl back to the Ozarks to be swaddled in family commotion. Or perhaps return to my childhood roots in Chicago. Maybe I should allow myself to be pulled to another extreme, to Miami to be with Luke, my first love and first kiss from eighth grade. After our recent reunion, I worried that by walking my butt and hard-earned degree onto this flight in search of a fat paycheck at sea I might miss out on a chance at a real career—and maybe love—on land. And yet, no other promising option presented itself after living in Seattle for nine months.

In line and ready to board the plane, I overheard a guy say, "I'm getting on this flight no matter what. My brother just got killed up there." I turned to my new best friend Stephanie looking for either a kick in the pants or a sign that we should turn back—as if we needed another sign. Unwavering, she said, "This is only the beginning, Girlfriend!" A kick in the pants it is. I didn't know then how this one choice would help loosen the stranglehold of my past and shape my future.

As we took our seats on the half-occupied, twin-prop plane, I said to Stephanie, "Next they'll haul us over the drop zone and expect us to jump out when the door swings open."

"Yeah, and we'll both do it, because we won't be called chickens," she replied. "Right?" We scanned each other's grimaces for some encouragement.

The oversized vinyl seats provided ample legroom, and as I stretched out I noticed the stained ashtrays in the arm rests and the missing chips of paint on the speckled wall. This plane had probably been kicked around since the 1940s, when Reeve Aleutian Air first flew to Dutch Harbor. Call me chicken, but I hoped its maintenance was up to date.

Hours earlier, on the first leg of my flight, the pilot out of Seattle's SeaTac airport had said, "There isn't a prettier place to fly out of on a clear day than Seattle." I'd left behind the first signs of spring: temperatures in the '50s, mountain snow melting into river valleys and streams, the bright fluorescence of new shoots, and the scent of cherry blossoms and hyacinths breaking through the wet earth. I'd looked out the airplane window over the evergreen hillsides, surrounding waters, and the Cascade Mountains. The captain reaffirmed my decision. That beauty. *That* is another reason why I'd left Missouri behind for Seattle. Now I aimed for the unknowns of Alaska.

Leaving Anchorage, I caught a last glimpse of civilization as it disappeared behind continuous white peaks of a different range, the Chugach Mountains. Perched on the edge of my seat, I contemplated this new adventure to Dutch Harbor—800 miles southeast of Russia, 846 air miles southwest of Anchorage on Unalaska Island at the end of the Aleutian Peninsula. Dutch, like Hawaii, is included in The Chain—volcanic islands making up part of the ominous sounding Ring of Fire that surrounds the outer Pacific Rim. Unlike Hawaii, there would be no palm trees, luaus, hula dances, or floral leis upon my arrival. In less than two hours, we'd be standing at the edge of the subarctic tundra.

An hour into the flight, Stephanie and I, the only two women passengers, sat silent, too nervous to speak and too macho to admit it. The roar of the twin engines magnified my fears. I searched for assurance in the glazed eyes of the guy with flushed cheeks and a rusty Brillo pad beard sitting across from me. Another sat folded in his seat with a stocking cap pulled down over his bushy hair to his wide-open mouth. A guy about my age, in sweatpants and a hooded sweatshirt, snored and overflowed into the aisle. The men had scattered and passed out like dead fish after consuming a day's worth of alcohol in one morning of travel. Soon I'd be eating, sleeping, and working side by side with guys like these.

I was assigned to the F/V *Nomad*, a 141-foot freezer longliner that fished with fixed gear by hook and line at different depths to target Pacific cod, black cod (sablefish), turbot, and rockfish. She was only one of more than 300 commercial fishing vessels and twenty shore-side processing plants to carry an observer at some point during the Alaskan fishing season. Vessels between sixty and 125 feet required an observer only 30 percent of the time; larger vessels had 100 percent coverage, and smaller boats were exempt. I could have been assigned to a shoreside processing plant or a "Mothership," a giant ship tied in the bay that accepts and processes fish from other catcher-only vessels. Catcher trawlers fished midwater or on the ocean bed with a net, and without factories aboard, they held their fish for days on refrigerated seawater until they were delivered to a shoreside plant or a Mothership for processing. As a first-time observer, I would avoid being selected to be on a crabber, which has a short season with high risk; I'd need more experience and my sea legs first. Like Stephanie, I could have been assigned to a big ol' factory trawler that caught groundfish by dragging a net across the seafloor. Their catch, like ours, would be processed, packed, and frozen onboard. With each of our trips lasting weeks, possibly months, there wasn't much chance that Stef and I would return to Dutch Harbor at the same time.

While positive affirmations—such as "No fear!"—ballooned in my head, the bad weather was upon us. The pilots were rumored to be Vietnam vets, experts in the art of landing on tiny jungle air-strips, but I hoped we wouldn't need their unique talents this day. My stomach twisted like taffy, and a volcano of bile upwelled in my stomach. I had not yet mastered the appearance of bravery and con-fidence. I moved to an empty row in the back of the plane, where only a barf bag tucked into the seatback pocket comforted me. My eyes closed tight, and my muscles stiffened through the turbulence as I prepared for the downward thrust of this roller coaster ride. Would seasickness be worse?

We descended through clouds stacked between the frozen hill-sides. I scanned the gloom for a bandage strip runway and envi-sioned us crash-landing in the water before I'd ever have a chance to sink on my fishing vessel. My grip on the armrests tightened; I tensed as if I were sitting in the dentist's chair and he was coming at me with the drill. The harrowing succession continued: fog, white-capped black water bound by cliffs, then, slam! My belt tightened like a noose around my stomach and my face jerked toward the seat in front of me. The wings tipped side to side as we skated at an angle to a smoking halt. We stopped short of the end of the airstrip, where asphalt met angular piles of rock down the slope to icy water. Held breaths released upon touchdown, followed by applause from the liquored up but well-seasoned passengers. The pilot, giddy from avoiding a crash, crackled over the speaker, "Welcome to the wild west of Dutch Harbor, Alaska!" Population 3,000.

My drunken companions stumbled out the tail exit of the plane, and I wondered if I'd have to share a room with any of them. Stef and I jumped into the cold and planted our feet on mud-laden rock that may as well have been the moon. Surrounding us was more rock . . . and water—water from the sky, water in our eyes, and rivulets on the gravel road running into puddles. I looked for the highest point, Makushin, an active volcano on the island, but cloud cover blunted its peak. I had woken up in Seattle, one of the country's hippest cities, and now I stood shivering in a small outpost on the Aleutians, one of the last major wilderness areas in North America. Stephanie and I walked side by side with our arms draped over each other's shoulders like security blankets. I leaned into her and said, "We're going to cry every day."

Our observer coordinator, who was stationed in a community bunkhouse in Dutch, greeted us outside the rustic airport. His fogged up John Denver glasses were the only thing visible beneath his bangs and layers of hoods. Six inches of mud caked our neoprene boots, gluing us upright against the horizontal rain and sleet. Rugged. Bare. Frozen. Gray. Desolate. The laughter, excitement, and anticipation Stephanie and I had shared were gone. Despite how terrified we felt, we gave each other the it's-going-to-be-okay look.

The coordinator helped us load the eighty-plus pounds of equipment we each were carrying into the bed of a pickup. My sampling gear—rubber gloves; two scales; a five-inch thick manual; data sheets; tally-counters; fish, bird, and mammal identification books; clipboards; a bottle of oil (to help prevent rust on the equipment); glass vials and preservative; a measuring tape; a small bucket; scalpels; and a calculator—along with my sleeping bag and rain gear, was packed in two blue laundry baskets that were roped together. Our dread mounted when he said, "Hop in," and we realized he meant "Hop in the back" and not the warm, dry cab. (Say goodbye to comfort.) We hurdled the pickup's tailgate and sat in the bed with our gear for the coldest five minutes we'd ever spent.

Before we could wrap our minds around our new situation, we were dropped between two freshly painted blue ships. Stef would be first to board her vessel. It was a black, dented 186-foot factory trawler—not the shiny luxury yacht I'd somehow envisioned. Only the fierce wind and sleet forced us onto the deck, a junkyard of clanging metal. We dodged piles of netting and oddball gear, while spying eyes watched us from dark shadows. Stef's main worry had been the crew's confrontational reputation she'd heard about from other observers. But seeing her boat now, she had a bigger concern. "Laura, this sucker is gonna sink. It's too rusty to be seaworthy."

As we grew closer to abandoning Stef on her crap-trap vessel, I thought, *We (I) needed a more gradual transition, a segue.* Oh God, help me. The rush to the airport, to the next plane, to the back of a pickup, only to be directly dropped off at some honkin' heap of metal was too much. Stef's room was not yet ready for her to check in, so we waited in the galley. Within minutes, a stubbly faced crewman handed her a bottle of Windex and a box of dryer sheets and said, "Here. It's for the odor in your room." We were both speechless as we realized this was the real deal. How could we ever have prepared for this and still think it was a good idea? I thought back to our training class and our hell-and-brimstone instilling instructor. We had three weeks of exaggerations to weed out the wimps, right? No, it really was that bad. As I exited the galley, Stef stared back at me over her shoulder as if handcuffed and hogtied in an orange jumpsuit, exiting a courtroom after being given a lifetime sentence. Poor Stephanie. Poor *me*; my sentencing was next.

Back in the bed of the pickup, its tires kicked up chunks of mud and gravel as we jerked through potholes and curved around the wave-battered shoreline to another industrial dock and group of vessels. I dumped my gear over the tailgate and looked up at the bow before me, which displayed a different name than the one I'd been assigned. A lump swelled in my throat, and a wave of panic engulfed me as I said to the observer coordinator, "Wait. This isn't the *Nomad*!" I was mentally prepared to be on one type of vessel, but I knew I could be tossed onto another at the last minute.

Holding his hood in place, the coordinator shouted over the howling wind, "Out there!" and pointed toward the water. To my surprise, there she was—count 'em—the *third* boat from shore.

With limited dock space to accommodate the many vessels, they were tethered together, port to starboard, extending out into the bay. My ship's dark blue hull peeked out from behind the two closer vessels like a shy child. I was relieved to be on my assigned vessel, but had no idea how I would I manage the transfer with all my gear in this crappy weather. It was time to take off the training wheels and get a big push onto the freeway.

Jumping from boat to boat was not mentioned in training, so it had never registered on my list of concerns. What else hadn't I thought about in advance? Determined to not look like a wuss, I confronted the obstacle course with the confidence of a boot camp rookie. Each vessel swayed to its own bucking rhythm, cushioned by the squeeze and release of the round buoys sandwiched between them. The three-foot voids seemed like chasms, too wide to hurdle safely, even with webbed cargo nets hanging between the frigid thirty-six-degree water and me. The crewmen in front of me crossed without hesitation; those behind me waited as I paused. Like a line of busy worker ants, we carried our surplus back to the nest. Though I wanted to hunker down in defeat, I shrugged off the frozen sleet, heaved my gear onto the railing, and leapt across the first gap. I would conquer the other two crossings like any difficulty in life, one at a time.

After the second successful crossing, a tall crewman with dark skin and large hands said, "Let me help you." He grinned and traded me his box of lettuce for my burdensome gear. I wondered if I'd just dropped a few rungs on the ladder of respect. I'd learned to do for myself instead of asking for help from others, fearing they'd be put out. Was this crewman chivalrous, or did he think I couldn't do it? I stumbled with each step, but managed to coax the produce over the final rail. How much heavier would fish be than lettuce? With my feet firmly planted on my boat, I'd entered the ultimate masculine world.

The bitter cold stung my lungs as I surveyed the outside of the ship. A white foremast, a beanstalk ladder leading to a cluster of lights, and a massive black crane dominated the bow like a giant yin and yang. I was now the shy one, hiding behind the box of greens. The uppermost deck held a confusing network of smokestacks, lights, radar domes, and antennas. The middle deck held javelin-like aluminum poles (buoy markers), slanted and layered into white PVC pipes attached to the railing; pink buoys tied together like balloons; and other equipment unfamiliar to my amateur eyes. Most importantly, I spotted the bulky, white-washed cases containing the life rafts. I would not forget their location.

I entered the starboard door with caution as a few crew members squeezed by. One seized my crate, and I could swear he licked his lips—and not because he loved raw vegetables. Another, Dean, with seductive green eyes and a captivating smile, leaned with one knee bent against the wall outside my room, eager to greet the new female aboard. I felt like a juicy, USDA prime steak as Dean, the deck boss, showed me my quarters.

He removed the grimy baseball cap he wore backwards, rubbed his balding head, and said, "Here's your stateroom."

It was more locker room than stateroom. I whiffed the stale air and dropped my duffel bag and backpack. The tiny space had dull brown indoor-outdoor carpeting, alder-toned paneling, and four bunks, commonly called "racks." Merriam-Webster's Dictionary defines a rack as "an instrument of torture on which a body is stretched." That's pretty close; or maybe "a shelf" is a more apt description. I would soon be sleeping on a shelf.

Dean flexed his biceps as he put his hat back on, smacked the bunk on his way out, and said, "You get this one above Jazz. He's the cook. He snores. He snores and *farts*. A *lot*." He added with a wink, "If you can't sleep, I'm down the hallway on the left."

"Um, thanks. I have earplugs. I'll be fine," I said. "But can you direct me to the bathroom?" Like a puppy, scared, excited, and overwhelmed in its new environment, I could have peed my pants.

"You mean the head? Well, since you're the only woman aboard, you'll share one with the two engineers. Go through their room, which is on the right," he winked at me again. "Opposite my room." All directions from Green Eyes would be in reference to where his room was located, so there was no confusion in case I wanted to visit him among his seven roommates. I had landed on a singles cruise and just discovered I was the only woman who had signed up.

"Half the battle is getting there," they say. My voyage had begun at sunrise, when the taxi dropped me and Stef at SeaTac Airport. Curbside, I had unloaded my duffel bag full of Army Surplus and Goodwill supplies, all I'd need to blend in with the crew: oversized flannel shirts, hooded sweatshirts, baggy sweatpants, and a winter Army jacket. Next to the duffel bag sat my two laundry baskets on wheels, lashed together and waiting to be pulled, like a little blue wagon on a rope leash.

I wheeled my geek gear to the Alaska Airlines terminal. The long line of fishermen eyed me and my absurd load. I might as well have been wearing a clown costume.

Single and just twenty-four years old, men were always vying for a larger space in my mind. I scouted the lineup for any cute guys. I knew if I was ever to have a serious relationship, I needed to surround myself with exceptional men, those I'd consider marrying—probably those found on land. I didn't think fishermen were my type, but neither were some of my recent interests. The Greek restaurateur with the refined palate who often took me to dinner was too short. The hiker from the South was overly polite and spoke with a little too much sing-song in his voice. The hard-bodied, African American banker and bouncer, who gazed at himself in every window, was stacked with muscles as well as serious debt. The preacher's son spent his daily word quota crooning in his music recording studio with few left for me. Then there was Luke, the real estate entrepreneur in Florida, who always had a place in my heart. I wondered if he would be right for me now. Perhaps going out to sea would rid me of dates born from flattery, loneliness, and love of the idea of being in love, but without any future potential.

I came close to settling once the year before I moved to Seattle. He was a former high school heartthrob who was living in the Chicago area while I studied in Missouri and ventured to Maine on a summer research scholarship. His feelings then progressed faster than mine in the year, and he moved to Seattle because of my plan to go there, despite my rejection of his one-carat ring and proposal. His arms no longer made me feel safe. His eyes didn't hold mine when we kissed. My heart no longer jumped when we embraced. Our flame reignited and burned briefly. By the time I moved to Seattle, I was relieved to learn that his restless self and the diamond ring were headed in another direction . . . to Utah to be with a new girlfriend.

Couldn't I find a good man, or did I avoid long-term relationships by dating the wrong men? Or were men put in my path to distract me from my goals? My mom encouraged me to be independent, telling me, "Make your own money first," and "Be able to take care of yourself. Don't wind up being dependent on a man." I set aside my desire to find love and focused on finding a career. Maybe Alaska would teach me some lessons about life and love. Sea would be a place to clear my head, for surely I'd never be interested in a fisherman.

Now, after a day of being tossed between taxis, planes, trucks, and ships, I knew most of the battle was still ahead. I stood in my empty stateroom waiting for my thoughts to catch up with my unbelievable reality.

Looking at my gear pile, I hoped I didn't forget anything. There would be no running to the store at sea. One thing I knew not to forget was my bulky red gumby survival suit, which was pushing out from the grates of my baskets. The night before, I'd waxed the stiff zipper again and again to be sure it was functional. Then I slithered into it, put up the hood, and zipped it. I repeated this procedure multiple times to ensure I could do it in under a minute, like we're supposed to do. I might not have felt completely secure with all my other duties at this time, but I was confident on how to get into that sucker. Fast. My life depended on it.

Slowly, I unpacked and jammed my clothes into two drawers and a gym locker of a closet. Royal blue curtains, providing my only source of privacy, were strung along my rack. I wrapped a clean sheet around the flimsy mattress pad, unrolled my flannel-lined sleeping bag, and shoved my gumby suit into the dim corner of the three-by-seven-foot bunk. The coffin-like space was all mine. Now, if only someone would bring me some Windex and dryer sheets.

We were still docked shoreside, but soon we'd face unrelenting wind, snow, ice, and squalls of mountainous waves. Despite my three weeks of training, I still felt as if I'd been plucked from a picture in a handbook and dropped onto a real-life commercial fishing boat, not knowing what living with these fishermen would really be like. There was nothing for me to do. I had no responsibilities until we started to catch fish, but we'd have to travel a day or more to reach the fishing grounds. I contemplated getting off the boat to call someone and freak out, but the boat was leaving as soon as the groceries were aboard, and I had no idea where to find a payphone anyway. Plus, I wasn't too eager to practice my long jump between vessels again. There was no hand to reach out and hold me up and no turning back from this boatload of men.

I was caught in a force between the moon and sun, like the ocean tide, steadily shoving me away, while simultaneously trying to drag me back to shore. Now, I'd been pushed even farther away from family and the life I aspired to on land, to the edge of the world it seemed, where I might just fall off the horizon.

All I wanted to do was curl up in my bunk with my loyal friend, my journal, turn off the lights, and never leave. But I had to learn my way around the ship . . . and the guys. I guess it was time to put on a brave face and mingle.

2

THE TOUR

WITHIN hours of boarding, I met the captain. I assumed he'd be a loner, comfortable with isolation. I knew they spent most of their time solo, at the helm. Would he be an antisocial recluse, a brokenhearted poet, or a gnarly dictator? As I entered the wheelhouse, he hung up the radio, turned around, and cast me a white smile, from dimple to dimple, beneath his thick mustache, "Hello. I'm Captain Gabe."

Hmmm. Kinda Marlboro Man handsome. I was pleased to see he wasn't what I'd expected: a wrinkled, thick-skinned, scratchy-throated man with a mane, yellow slicker, and a missing finger, like I'd seen on the frozen fish stick commercials. His outgrown hair indicated he'd been at sea for at least a month or two, but the sparkle in his sapphire eyes and pleasant tone told me he was in good spirits.

"Welcome to *The Love Boat*," he said. "Have you seen the ship yet? I'll give you a quick tour." I had considered being a cruise director, like Julie on *The Love Boat*, but this was no cruise ship. Gabe motioned me toward the stairs, "After yo*uuu*, D*uuu*de." He was about ten years older than me, but used the lingo of a teenage surfer fresh off a California beach.

"Speaking of dudes. How many dudes are we talking here?" I asked.

"Twenty-five, including myself," he answered. "Unless someone quits before we leave the bay. Which is entirely possible."

It would be full-on all men—all the time.

Space was limited on a ship half the size of a football field. A narrow hallway split the thirty-foot beam of the vessel starboard to port. We started the tour at the galley in the stern of the ship. Two tables were covered in green grippy net and bordered by a wooden lip. Centerpiece sectionals held napkins, salt, pepper, ketchup, hot sauce, syrup, salad dressing, and anything else that could roll or take flight during bad weather. Plastic baskets of VHS videos—probably more along the lines of *The Terminator* and *Aliens* than *When Harry Met Sally*—teetered on the end of one table. Staying optimistic, I assumed no X-rated films were aboard. Next to the recirculating iced tea and red punch dispenser hung a bookcase of tattered paperbacks, mainly sci-fi and legal thrillers. I anticipated lots of grunting, swear words, peacock struts, chest-beating, and arm punches under a swirling cloud of cigarette smoke in this space. The clock ticked away the minutes above an empty corkboard. Would there ever be a notice or news to post at sea?

The kitchen was equipped with the usual commercial appliances: stove, refrigerator, deep sink, and dishwasher. Everything was tied, bolted, or glued down, which clearly indicated that every day would be like living through an earthquake. Bungee cords were not on my gear list, but scanning the galley, they should have been. Jumbo cans and spice containers lined the counters. I zeroed in on the wide selection of oversized knives, secretly hoping no ex-cons were aboard. Little did I know that many fishermen worked at sea as a condition of Huber, a temporary prison work-release program.

They're free to work at sea or go back to jail. I wondered if being cooped up on a boat for three months, with nowhere to roam, might feel like jail. Still, I was lucky. The unadorned vessel was only a few years old and freshly painted. This might be as good as it could get.

A chipper voice perked up over the Boyz II Men cassette playing on the boombox. A black man with a bulkie roll figure hidden by a white crossover collar chef shirt introduced himself, "Hello. I'm Jazz. I'm the cook, housekeeper, and chief bull-shitter. I guess we're roommates, too." His undereye bags, purple and swollen as if he had two shiners, creased while he informed me, "Your laundry day is Wednesday. Put it in a bag with your name and throw it in the laundry room by 7:00 a.m." He pointed to the small landing down the stairs from the galley. My first thought was: *Wow, what luxury. Someone is going to cook my food and do my laundry.* But then I realized, *my snoring, farting roommate is going to wash, fluff, and fold my bras and underwear!* I expected every man aboard to know all the details of my undergarments, right down to the percentage of cotton, by nightfall on laundry day. I could hear it now, "Yes, shipmates, the observer wears Jockey bikinis and French cuts in solids and stripes." And, more embarrassing, "Her B-cup Maidenform bras have "Precious Littles" written on the tags!" My underwear might as well be raised up the mast and displayed—a flag of surrender. Suddenly, I was glad that I left my lacey and racy collection behind.

Then, a horrifying thought hit me: *What about my monthly?* Accidents were bound to happen within the next three full moons. Where would I rinse and dry my skivvies? In the head I had to share with two engineers? Dangle them off the blue curtain on my rack, face-to-cotton-panel with my three male roommates? I couldn't toss *those* in the wash for Jazz to casually discuss around the galley table. If I jettisoned them overboard instead, I pictured them dragged up by fishing gear, like a stray message in a bottle. This was one of those things I hadn't thought about in advance.

The tour continued. Captain Gabe showed me other staterooms, all the same wall-to-wall brown, differing only in the number of bunks—two, four, or eight. He then ordered two crewmen to haul my cumbersome sampling gear down the steep metal grid stairs to the processing factory. As the captain led me through rows of ogling eyes, I greeted each one like I was petitioning votes for Prom Queen, hoping to gain their favor. He introduced me to the first mate, Hobey, who worked opposite Captain Gabe's shift. Hobey wore a baseball hat over his Billy Ray Cyrus achy-breaky mullet and a grin that was a combination of Cheshire cat and an actual catfish. Although he seemed nice enough, he doused himself with Patchouli. I told the captain that it reminded me of the anal gland musk of poodles—a scent I became all too familiar with while working at a veterinary clinic. "Yeah, well, he thinks chicks dig it," he explained.

The crew included all varieties, except for the female kind. Extreme weather and fishing probably attracted personalities that stood well outside the bell curve for normal. My decision to work here placed me out of the "normal" range, too.

I wasn't entirely clueless about what it would be like as the sole woman aboard ship. My senior year of high school, when I moved from Chicago to the Ozarks of Missouri, I was the new girl, fresh bait, the city slicker plopped into a small town, and the only female in shop class. I hoped this wasn't a throwback to high school, where I'd felt like a conquest. With twenty-five guys aboard, I knew there could be some attraction, but fraternizing or "physical or emotional involvement," was *highly discouraged* in training.

"Oh, I can see you're going to get a lot of attention," Captain Gabe said at the base of the stairs to the wheelhouse. "Even though you're the only woman aboard, an attractive woman I must say, they're harmless. It's me you have to look out for." Unsure if he was joking, I was both flattered and frightened. What else would I have to be on the lookout for?

"Okay, I gotta go run this ship," he said. "You're on your own from here."

Not yet ready to explore on my own, I headed back to my room—my safe zone.

Though my mind-set was to expect the unexpected, I was unprepared for what was to come next. I knocked on the closed door of my room. "Hello. Is anyone in there?" I asked.

"Yeah! Yeah!" said a scratchy voice. "Come in."

I cracked open the door and edged my way in until my eyes bulged out at the bulge staring back at me. Roommate number two, standing proud and hairy-chested with nothing on but white briefs.

"How's it goin'?" he asked casually, acting unstirred.

It's my first day aboard, and I'm already looking at a strange man, my roommate nonetheless, in his underwear! It was no accident. He seemed to revel in making me uncomfortable.

I wanted to tell him off, but instead I snatched my yellow Walkman and cassettes from the closet. As I strolled out past Fruit-of-the-Loom in his one-man panty parade, I fixed my eyes on the slanted patch pocket, front and center of his pelvis, and heckled, "Is *that* supposed to impress me?" I stared him down like an animal vying for territory. I marched out the door like a boxer leaving the ring after a TKO. The complexity of my situation was becoming clearer.

Before arriving on board, I never thought much about where I'd sleep or who'd wash my undergarments. I was used to guy behavior, with communications short and to the point. I assumed the crew would act like a houseful of brothers, like my own. Except for the guy norm of leaving the toilet seat in the up position, why should gender matter? I assumed the unwritten rules still applied:

- Clean up after yourself.

- Don't leave the lights on.
- Be quiet when someone is sleeping.
- Wear *pants*!

That's it. But after my close encounter with Underwear Man, I realized I'd have to figure out the "norms" on a fishing boat. I had ventured to the other side and was clearly in Man's Land now.

3

DEPARTURE

BLACK floats wrapped with rows of rubber tires bumped between our vessels. Russian men, with serious eyes and gold teeth, stood on the deck of the adjacent ship in their warm fur hats. Before heading to the fishing grounds—north of the Pribilof Islands, "The Pribs"—we made a twelve-hour *pit stop* to offload the product from the previous trip onto a 400-foot Russian tramper, an international fish taxi, anchored in the bay. I watched as cranes swung pallets of frozen fish over the cargo net and then lowered them into the tramper's freezer hold below deck. Two of their crewmen guided the cable; one of them flipped me off. Nice! The tramper would haul the catch to Japan, where it would be held in cold storage and then redistributed or auctioned to the highest bidder.

Our crewmen hung over the railing with their arms outstretched, waving cartons of cigarettes at the Russian men. "Hey, you! You want?" they yelled, their eyes gleaming at the Russians' prized pelts perched on their heads. Neither party understood the foreign chatter, but the message was clear: several cases of American smokes in exchange for Russian fur hats. Minutes later, Dean with his inviting green eyes and a burnt stub of a cigarette in his mouth, wheeled around the corner. He proudly offered me an official, well-worn, oil-stained, Russian hat as if he'd won me a stuffed animal at the county fair. The luring of the new girl had begun.

When the Russian tramper released our lines, I made my way onto the deck, where I was met with wind, sleet, and popcorn-size hail. This was no salt and seaweed facial. I thought this must be what it feels like to be run through a carwash. Through the fog I could see a blur of lights from buildings, pickup trucks, and docked boats. It might be weeks or even months before I saw another shoreline. What would it be like *out there*, in unprotected waters? Growing up in the Chicago area, if anyone had said that someday I'd be working on a fishing boat on the Bering Sea, my response might've been an echo of my mom's, "When Hell freezes over!" Maybe that's exactly where I was headed. Our fishing grounds were fifteen to twenty hours and 200 miles away.

I didn't see the ocean until I was in high school. My imagination, books, Jacques Cousteau programs, and downtown Chicago's Shedd Aquarium had been my only connection to the sea. On that first encounter, I dipped my toes into the Atlantic Ocean at Myrtle Beach, South Carolina. The saltwater held me light and buoyant above the foamy surf. I wanted to learn about the world beneath me and beyond what I could see or fathom. That was the moment I knew that living and working near water would be essential to my happiness.

While other high school girls were flirting with guys at parties, I spent Friday nights on the southwest side of Lake Michigan at the Waukegan Harbor breakwater. I dragged along my resistant friend, who said like a Doctor Seuss rhyme, "I'd rather sit in a box than here on these rocks." Those jagged rocks were my imaginary island, from which I pierced the darkness in search of the unseen other side. I wondered what it was like at sea—really at sea, when you're surrounded by water, sky, and a few of God's creatures to remind you that you're not alone. Lake Michigan, more than twenty times larger than Washington's Puget Sound, was my ocean, my channel to somewhere else.

Seven years later, there I stood on a 141-foot floating mass of steel leaving the Aleutian Islands, the southern boundary of the Bering Sea. An extension of the Pacific Ocean, the Bering Sea is the eighth largest sea in the world. We would be fishing somewhere in the 878,000 square miles between Alaska and Russia in a variety of ocean terrain: a shallow continental shelf; gradual slopes; or above the edge of deep canyons that plummet into the abyss. Only the wild was ahead of me—not the kind you bounce in and out of while hiking, car camping, or driving through a wildlife park with your windows down. I was heading 200 miles offshore into blizzards and hurricane-force winds, to that *somewhere else* I'd dreamt about as a teenager on the shores of Lake Michigan, where if you hold a fish out the window, it gets bitten off by a Steller sea lion or an orca whale. It doesn't get any wilder than that.

Within hours of departing the Russian tramper, Captain Gabe called a mandatory safety drill in the galley, where all eyes were on me, except for the two pairs on deck barfing over the railing. Their retching made my own guts quiver, and I hoped I wouldn't get linked into a chain reaction. The captain explained what to do in case of a fire, a man overboard, or worse, if the ship went down. The men's survival suits were located a level above us, in an outside locker near the life rafts; I would sleep with mine like a teddy bear. Sitting there, sandwiched between two crewmen, I gritted my teeth and gripped the galley bench tighter against the rolling, twisting surge beneath the vessel. We had pulled past the sheltered islands into wider channels and open, deeper waters. Soon we'd face waves big enough to capsize a boat.

"No drugs or alcohol are allowed aboard this ship," Captain Gabe said with serious brows. "If I hear about it, consider yourself fired."

Waving his clipboard at us, he continued, "Look out for each other, and keep your hands and feet out of coils!" I pictured runaway hooks baited with squid and loops of line wrapped around my leg, dragging me like a human anchor through the ice-cold water down to the ocean floor.

When he told us, "Don't throw a damn thing overboard unless you can eat it!" I envisioned buoyant garbage—plastic bottles and orange rubber gloves—floating in our wake, and me writing the infraction in my logbook.

"We have a diverse crew, so I don't want to hear any racist shit!"

Seated around me were Japanese, Vietnamese, Mexicans, Blacks, Samoans, and a mixture of other cultures, including the lean white guy with blonde mini-ponytails perched on top of his head who definitely wasn't from the US. He didn't know it yet, but he'd already signed up for a whupping just because of the way he wore his hair. As diverse as we were, we had one thing in common: we chose the extreme.

Then the focus shifted to me as Captain Gabe ordered the crew, "Keep porno magazines and videos out of sight while our female observer is aboard." I kept my gaze on him. "Treat her with respect. Serve her. Help her in whatever she requests. If she asks you to kiss her ass, you ask 'Where?' and pucker up! You can also tone down the F-bombs."

Although I admired his straightforward demands—I didn't want to be treated as "less than"—I had no expectations of seeing the gentler side of this bunch, or for them to alter their behavior for me. Though maybe, just maybe, the guys would act a little nicer, try a little harder, and avoid blatant crotch scratching, belching, or farting in front of me. I kept a stoic front while all eyes stared at me, a flower in a field of thistles.

Sitting among the crew, I wondered what else I'd encounter in the next three months with all the hidden porn and testosterone booming through the vessel, contained only by the pounding surf outside. This was my fresh start, day one of a ninety-day contract, Bering Sea boot camp. The waves grew larger and my new home, my new world, instantly became smaller.

That evening, before bed, I stood on deck, face to the wind. I bent over the railing and searched deep into the water for signs of life. A person could technically drown in two inches of water in a bathtub, but this was different. Here you would reach out into the cold emptiness and no one would be there to pull you up; I'd felt that way a lot in life. A nearly full moon floated in the dark sky like a crystal ball, but empty, void of any future predictions. It cast an iridescent halo on the clouds below. Was someone on land looking at the same moonlight and thinking of me? I hoped so. As the distance between me and the land increased, I felt both lost and affirmed. I survived my entry into shipboard life. This was the starting line, and I was committed to the course.

Later, wrapped in a flannel cocoon, I stretched out in my rack for my first attempt at slumber on this carnival ride atop the Bering Sea. I'd never slept on a boat that wasn't anchored or tied to a dock, where I could abort ship if something went wrong in the night. I thought back to the cold-water survival drill in Seattle, where I'd stood at the edge of Lake Washington dressed in my bulky red immersion suit like an awkward aquatic superhero. At the shout of, "Go!" I jumped into the flat, calm lake and pretended to be overboard in the Bering Sea. The hooded suit, thick and cumbersome, squeezed tight against my body and pushed the warm air up through the seal around my face; the escaping air would be replaced with thirty-five-degree water seeping in. But I was in the lake, flailing in a buoyant awkward backstroke for fifty meters to the inflatable, igloo-style life raft. On the ocean, I'd be lucky if I could even spot the raft while being sucked and pulled and blown against raging waves and wind.

During the drill, I struggled to pull my body onto the raft. As my feet crossed the threshold, the horn sounded. Among my clapping classmates I heard a "Woohoo, Girlfriend!" from Stef, my personal cheerleader and voice of reason.

But as I laid in my bunk, there was no Stef to help me overcome my doubts and relieve the churning in my stomach. All I could think about were the enormous white-capped waves, the force of transient water and wind against solid steel, the dull pounding, and the constant rise and fall. Logically, I knew ships were constructed to float, to voyage, to shelter against the unforgiving ocean and weather. Still, I took little comfort in knowing what was between me and the ferocity of the sea: three-eighths-inch plates of steel, a few beams, and fuel tanks. I thought of how dark and far it was to the bottom of the ocean and how cold the water must feel on a warm, trembling body.

I prayed to God wholeheartedly and recited the escape route in my head. If the time came, I would put on my red survival suit, stumble out the galley door to the stern deck, pull myself up the slippery rungs of a ladder, and aim for the life raft. Would I be able to open the case? I couldn't depend on one of the guys to do it for me. Maybe I would have to plummet thirty-plus feet into the ocean and swim to the raft, which would have likely tumbled away in the wind and waves like a beach ball.

When I signed on, commercial fishing ranked as the single most deadly occupation. According to the Centers for Disease Control and Prevention, between 1991 and 1992 in Alaska, seventy fatalities occurred to commercial fishermen—twenty times the overall US occupational fatality rate—almost half of those in the Bering

Sea. The cause of death for the majority was drowning or presumed drowning due to hypothermia. If our ship sunk, we'd likely die within minutes of immersion. The survival suit would keep us alive long enough for us to know that we were dying, the last seconds spent in prayer and panic.

I turned up the acoustic guitar music in my headphones to strum away and temper my growing list of fears. I said a prayer to quiet my brain.

"Dear God, please help me avoid barfing in my bunk, seeing another crewman in his underwear, and sinking today or any other day." I exhaled. "Oh, and one more thing, please help me figure out how to do my job. Amen."

4

ON THE MOVE

ALMOST ten months earlier, as a college graduate with a bachelor of science in biology and a minor in chemistry, the Show-Me State had shown me few prospects, low wages, and no way except the highway on which I drove west over 2,000 miles until I hit Seattle. The Emerald City promised curbside recycling, towering evergreens, salmon migrating through backyards, and I'd hoped a new life. My goals were simple: to be wedged between mountains and ocean, attend graduate school, and become some sort of *-ist*: scientist, biologist, ecologist. Led by a gut feeling and wanderlust, with no one to rely on and no Plan B, nothing stood between me and my future—hope came bursting through the open car windows. In my rearview mirror lay a life strung between a childhood in Chicago and senior year of high school through college in the Ozarks.

Growing up I'd felt responsible for my mom and my brother Tom, who is only fourteen months younger than me. I was the logical one, filling the role of fulcrum for my teeter-tottering family. Now in my absence, my stepdad, Walter, would have to be the grounding wire in my electrically charged family—or maybe we'd

all char and splinter and dissolve like sawdust. I felt guilty for abandoning them, like I was saving myself and leaving them helpless
inside a burning building. Despite the guilt and worry I carried,
I felt liberated to know our screaming matches and Mom's crying
jags would now be over the phone, buffered by distance. It seemed
easier to leave than to feel the jagged edges of the ever-widening
cracks between us.

How does one bundle up a life, a past, and leave it there—at
the curb like an old ratty couch bound for a dumpster? I was about
to find out.

Seattle, though exploding with prosperous opportunities for
dot-commers, rained hard on me and colored my green days gray.
All the doors I knocked on were sealed shut, only to be cracked
open for those with "more experience." Not to be deterred, I got
two part-time restaurant jobs and volunteered with a homeless
youth outreach group. I also worked a temporary field assistant
gig with a University of Washington graduate student. We waded
streams and clubbed spawned-out sockeye over the head just before
they died naturally to collect tissues for a genetic study. I had hoped
each thwap of a stick and limp carcass would be the gateway to a
graduate degree in fisheries, but after several months the adrenaline
vanished. I was left with only the strong silk thread of faith that
everything would somehow work out.

At last, the letter from UW's graduate program in fisheries
arrived. Sitting in my kitchen nook, I swiped my fingers over the
envelope's seal, too nervous to reveal my fate. I thought about the
opportunity I'd passed on—acceptance into the fisheries program
at the University of Arkansas, where a professor had offered me a
research assistant position studying tropical fish and coral reefs in
Hawaii. She had received her PhD from UW and knew my heart
and mind were set on Seattle. However, she tried to dissuade me like
a big sister. "It's a man's world there, and they're all salmonheads,"

she said. At the time, I knew nothing about salmon except how they looked on a plate and how they tasted. Despite her guidance, I refused a sure shot at grad school and plunged into the deep dark waters of uncertainty.

This was it, the moment I'd held out for. I ripped open the envelope and got a paper cut. Should this sting be taken as a warning? I slowly unfolded the bond paper and smoothed it out flat. The words on the page holding the key to my dreams. If the key didn't open the door, it wouldn't be the first time my dreams came to a dead halt.

Within weeks of graduating from high school I moved into a dumpy apartment an hour away from home. My goal was to work a year to save money and apply to veterinary college. As a kid, I wanted to be either a veterinarian or a garbage man, because they drove cool trucks and worked, so I thought, only one day a week when they retrieved our trash.

During my rigorous job search, most vet clinics turned me away. My experience with animals was limited to grooming horses and shoveling manure at the barn, feeding show dogs at a kennel, caring for the misfit critters in our own home, and dissecting fetal pigs in advanced biology class. I finally convinced one openhearted vet to hire me. I split my time and gasoline between his emergency hospital and two neighborhood clinics.

The job entailed regular pet maintenance: worming, vaccinations, filling prescriptions, cleaning ears and teeth, swabbing kennels, and assisting with routine surgeries. There was also a daily dose of trauma: death from disease and parasites, neglect from owners who could barely help themselves, and those pets we couldn't save. First thing each morning I'd visit the pets in quarantine, those with parvovirus, feline leukemia, or another illness, to see who made it through the night. I enjoyed the variety of working at three vet clinics, but the emergency hospital, with the more complex, challenging, and, unfortunately, most gruesome cases drew my interest most. The most difficult task for me was to euthanize an animal, stroking its fur and cradling it to provide comfort even as I felt the final heartbeat of its little triumphant spirit escaping the pain, going limp in my arms. My compassion was my downfall.

I hid my secret for an entire year. While I held a distressed dog, legs splayed on the counter, hit by a car with its tail split open, veins distended, and bleeding extensively, I'd ask a coworker, "Can you hold him for a minute? I need to go to the bathroom." I had to move fast to get into the bathroom, flip the light on, and close the door before, "Boom!" I passed out. Almost daily at the emergency clinic, I would wake up on the bathroom floor, slumped against the wall, my head having just missed hitting the toilet.

One afternoon at the clinic, I tucked a three-legged pug in my arms like a football. We'd amputated his broken leg—his little stub stitched like a patch on a rag doll. His bulging, watery eyes looked up at me as if asking, "What the heck just happened?" The doctor stood next to me, reaching above my head for a bottle of peroxide to remove the blood from his white smock. I turned to him and asked, "Doc, can you hold him for a minute?" I placed the pug on the counter. The room blurred. "It's really hot in here," I said. "Wow, it's really h-o" Bam!

I woke up on the floor, but this time in full view of the other assistants and my boss. The doctor hovered over me with a cold rag. I grasped for an explanation. Anemia. Low oxygen levels. I've been sick. He's a doctor; he'll call my bluff. "You okay?" he asked. I spent the night wondering.

The next morning, we talked over a Chow Chow's open chest, anesthetized and strapped to the operating table with a tube down his throat, his characteristic blue-black tongue dangling from the side of his mouth. The surgery part didn't faze me. The Chow's eyes were closed, so he couldn't look back at me. The doctor tilted his head, peered up over his bifocals and said, "Laura, you're a great assistant, and I care about you like a daughter." A light the size of a satellite dish shined over the operating table like an interrogation lamp. "I know your dream is to be a veterinarian, but your empathy is getting to you. You might consider another career."

He was right. I wasn't cut out for this work. He didn't fire me, but now I was without direction. Lost.

One of the other assistants recommended her alma mater, College of the Ozarks in Branson, Missouri. Students worked on campus in exchange for full tuition. It was known as Hard Work U. Hard Work was my middle name. I started classes that summer. I didn't know where a general biology degree would take me, but I loved the sciences. Despite never having lived near the ocean, I'd dreamt of careers that were beyond practical for a Midwesterner—becoming a dolphin trainer, a marine biologist, an oceanographer, or a cruise director. Classes in ecology and ichthyology, and a part-time job at the state hatchery, led me straight down a path toward slimy, wriggly fish, of all things.

At least fish were safe. Unlike pets at the vet clinic, I couldn't interact with them or interpret their body language or feelings. They didn't stare at me with teary eyes, or pant, or whimper, or have a voice. They just gaped and gazed out into space, just like I was gazing at the letter from UW back in my Seattle apartment—gulping for air and staring blankly at the word: *Unfortunately*.

All my hope and energy disappeared with that one word. Rejected. I was left bleeding, both literally and figuratively. Grad school was what I had been working toward; it was all I wanted. The words felt like a smash to the head, just like I'd done to those research salmon after their long journey upstream. Maybe the professor in Arkansas was right? What was I thinking? What would I do now?

The Ozarks tugged at me, urging my return. But that would verify that I'd made the wrong choice and I couldn't make it on my own. No way. No how. I'd stick it out and keep trying, at least for a while longer. After receiving a disappointing "B" on a project, my favorite college professor said, "Laura, it's not your grades, but your determination that will get you far in life." Believing in myself was the hard part.

I continued to club spawners with the UW salmonhead grad student who was obviously way smarter than me since he had been accepted. But the thrill was gone. Why was I working this part-time job now if it wasn't helping me bushwhack a path into grad school? I persisted in my search for a satisfying career and thus a satisfying life. I read the classifieds, typed cover letters, and applied for a plethora of "real" jobs, then anxiously checked the answering machine and eyed the phone, willing it to ring. Would employers keep me waiting like a guy who said he'd call? Between adding up my bills—rent, gas, insurance, food, taxes—I stole glimpses of the outside world through my window: buses carrying professionals to work and carefree couples dressed in GORE-TEX pushing their loaded strollers toward the Seattle Center and Space Needle.

By day, dressed in Red Robin's standard waitress uniform—red polo shirt, navy pleated pants or shorts, and greasy black shoes—I shuffled off to serve up gourmet burgers. By night, I changed into a pressed shirt to work as a hostess at Anthony's Home Port waterfront restaurant, where we served fish instead of me using my hard-earned biology degree to study or conserve them.

After a shift of answering to a cacophony of snapping fingers, whistles, and shouts of "Nice legs!" or "Hey, would ya take my burger order?" I cleared another table and shoved every dollar, quarter, dime, nickel, and penny into my pocket. As I wiped the spilled ranch dressing and slivered carrots off my shoes, it hit me. I can't do *this* anymore! Minimum wage wasn't enough compensation for my throbbing feet, the mind-numbing tedium of remembering if someone had ordered diet or regular soda, or the loss of my self-worth.

For whatever reason, an advertisement I'd seen almost a year earlier on my college's biology department bulletin board flashed in my mind: *Earn Fast Cash as a Fisheries Observer in Alaska.* I hadn't given the ad a second glance, thinking it was too extreme. Too far away. Too dangerous. Crazy even. Besides, I was headed for grad school (or so I thought), so I couldn't go to Alaska. But now it seemed the outrageous could be the answer, a break in the bad weather, a pot of gold at the end of a rainbow. With my head tilted up toward the sun, up above a layer of gray clouds, I saw the chance for a higher bank account balance.

The advertised $2,400-a-month to collect biological data on a commercial fishing boat felt like a million dollars compared to the four bucks per hour plus the measly tips I was earning. I was determined to work with fish, and serving them out of a deep fryer at a restaurant didn't count. I called an employer that contracted National Marine Fisheries Service (NMFS) certified observers. The North Pacific Groundfish Observer Program (NPGOP), the largest of six programs in the United States, began in 1990, though other diluted programs existed at the time. If hired, I would collect at-sea data for NMFS and the Alaska Department of Fish and Game (ADF&G), the agencies who managed fisheries in the Bering Sea, Gulf of Alaska, and the North Pacific. A skilled job for which I was qualified, and hopefully a step toward a career, it seemed like my best option. The walls of my tiny apartment stopped closing in on me.

During the initial phone interview, the contractor sold me the job with skulls and crossbones. "It's not for everyone," he said. "You'll likely be the only woman aboard, and you'll share a room with one to seven men. Most everyone smokes, so I hope that doesn't bother you. We're looking for someone who is mature, confident, and willing to work a three-month contract with the hope you'll extend. We invest a lot of time and money in training, so if you quit at the airport or the middle of your contract, you pay your way back from Alaska."

"There's no way I'd quit," I said. "My mom says I have the determination of a draft horse, if that tells you anything. And my work experiences and degree prove I'm capable."

It sounded good to my ears, but did I actually believe it? I kicked my slimy, black waitress shoes under the table like winged demons.

"Take a day or two to think about it, and call me if you're sure," he added, ending the conversation.

The work seemed to have all the components of life I enjoyed: the ocean, adventure, good pay, and the company of men. How could I refuse? But the job also included freezing temperatures, killer storms, and isolation from my friends and the world as I knew it.

That night in bed, I thought hard and prayed earnestly. Alone in the dark, with a head overflowing with thoughts, is when I'm usually my weakest, though this night I was briskly hiking up Mount Confidence. I knew this observer job would be way cooler and more amazing than any job in Seattle or college course. Losers don't go on adventures like this. Knowing every path has consequences, I chose to take a leap of faith and chose the mysterious, rugged wilderness of Alaska. This would either be my unconventional big break or my biggest mistake.

The next day, feeling like I was bungee-jumping off a cliff with a frayed line, my jittering fingers dialed the contractor: "When do I start?"

5

~~~~~~

LEAVING HOME

MY reasons for leaving Missouri had been compiling since childhood. The weeks before my move to Seattle, my family was exploding and tearing apart like fissures in the earth, knowing we needed
to live apart from one another. Still, we pulled together.

The day I left, Mom and I climbed into my midnight blue
Dodge Ram 50, dubbed "The Naked Truck" by college friends,
because I'd blown off the thin pin-striping with a power washer.
My stepdad, Walter, and my brother, Tom, were driving the U-haul
packed with the few domestic things I'd collected since high school.
We used CB radios to communicate between the two vehicles,
bringing back memories from my childhood when my mom would
talk on the CB to the truckers, locating accidents and speed traps
on the highways or "Bears in the air" at reported mileposts. Tom
and I would ask for the time: "Breaker, breaker 1-9 for a 10-36,
please." Now we joked to keep the tears at bay.

We traversed the Cascade Mountains to the I-90 bridge over
Lake Washington. As we passed beneath the tunnel entrance, the
curved arch read: "Seattle. Portal to the Pacific." It was right where I

wanted to be. Between the mountains and ocean is where I thought I'd find peace, away from the family drama, an anchor that had been dragging me down.

The four of us hauled my makings of a life up the four flights of marble stairs and into the 1939 studio apartment I had rented. My uncertainty and stress increased along with the record-high temperatures. Mom went straight to Chubby and Tubby's hardware store and bought a fan that blew in warm salt air mixed with the scent of curry from the Thai food restaurant across the alley. Then she proceeded to read the crime section of the newspaper out loud so I would know what I'd gotten myself into. Having a mom who had instilled street-smarts in me since I was a kid, I knew the police wouldn't be visiting *my* apartment anytime soon—there would be no incidents like the one at home just weeks before.

My apartment in Missouri had been packed away in boxes, and I was staying with Mom before my grand bon voyage to Seattle. Walter was in Chicago, but would soon return. I was excited about the possibilities ahead and had lined up hostess and waitress jobs. But there was uneasy quiver in my stomach. What if they changed their minds or laid me off after a short time?

My brother Tom was staying there, too. It was the first time we had stayed under the same roof since we rented a trailer together near campus for my first year of college. It wasn't fancy, but it was ours. Frequently I would arrive home late from studying or work to find drunk dudes strewn about the living room floor like Pick-Up Sticks. Our new beginning quickly ended. I couldn't help him; I had to help myself.

Now at my parents', Tom had been on a binger all week. He and a friend came home to raid the fridge in the wee hours. The kitchen was directly above Mom's bedroom, and he'd already gone into her bedroom to ask for a cigarette. You'd think he'd know better after more than twenty years under Mom's roof: don't wake Mom—ever—particularly before sunrise. Bad. Idea.

Growing up, Mom had kept us in line with a mixture of abundant hugs, I love you's, and recreational fun mixed with a daily vitamin of firm rules. She especially cited "Honor thy father and thy mother" from the Ten Commandments. She reminded us, "I'm not raising brats. You don't like my rules? Leave!" and "Shape up or ship out." And when we gave her any lip she'd show us her tight fist and say, "I brought you into this world, I'll knock you right out of it." We thought it was funny, but we also knew she meant business.

Often, I fantasized about being a cartoon hobo with a dirty face and a stick over my shoulder to carry my belongings wrapped up in a tight red sac. I liked how "I'm running away!" sounded. It was definitive—that is until Mom would retort: "I'll help you pack." I knew I couldn't leave my little brother behind. Back in his rebellious preteens, she would remind him, too, "If you can't follow my rules, you're going to military school. They'll teach you how to behave." When we complained of having too many chores, she'd say, "You can go live on a farm. Those kids are up at the crack of dawn. Farm kids know hard work." As if we didn't. She had rules; we followed them.

The sound of Mom pounding up the stairs to the kitchen could be heard throughout the house. I felt sick knowing my family was about to swing into full force dysfunction. I could gauge Mom's level of agitation by how hard she stomped. It was common for her to rant and pitch fits, but when she started stomping and fist pumping, someone was in serious trouble. This was the signal to all family members, including the dogs and cats, to retreat. Crawl under the bed. Close the door. Put on your headphones. Put your face in a book or under the blankets. Pretend you don't hear it. But this night I couldn't. I tailed Mom from a distance ready to step in to protect whoever needed protection.

Tom stood at the kitchen counter, a cigarette hanging from his mouth, making sandwiches. As kids we'd break Mom's cancer sticks in half and shove them back in the pack; or we'd jam them and my stepdad's cigars full with dime-store miniature explosives called loads. It didn't make them stop, but they thought twice before lighting up. Tom and I made a pact to never smoke, but there he stood puffing away like an exhaust pipe that had failed emissions.

Mom yelled, "You have money for booze, but not enough to buy yourself food or cigarettes?"

Tom, with his teeth gritted, responded, "Just leave me alone. Take a chill pill, Ma. Gosh." His face twisted, as he swallowed deep like a python taking down a small mammal, and the veins popped from his neck and forehead.

"Don't think you can come home and feed you and your friends anytime you want! Go. To. Bed!" You'd entered a war zone when she switched to one-word commands.

"Tom, please just put everything away." I pleaded. "Please go to bed. You're drunk. Your friend needs to leave."

He shouted back, "You're not the boss'a me!" We'd said this to each other since childhood, only this time no joke was implied.

For the first time as adults, my six-foot-two brother came at me like a bull, horns pointed directly at the red cape I wore in his mind. He shoved me. Hard. Sending me backwards. As I tried to push him back, he grabbed me and wrapped my arms around my neck. This wasn't the playful chokehold we'd used as kids, where one of us would say "I give" in defeat. Alcohol changed people, transforming those I loved into animals. I should have left him alone. He was bigger, stronger, and madder than I'd ever seen.

"Get. Out!" Mom yelled at him and his friend. Tom let me go. The sneer dropped from the friend's face, and he left, peeling out of the driveway. Still, my brother wouldn't budge from behind the counter.

Mom tried to phone the police, but Tom repeatedly hung up the phone before she could finish dialing. They resorted to throwing telephone books at each other. The yellow pages flapped and spun erratically through the air, like injured birds.

"That's it!" Mom stomped downstairs, the house shaking with each step. She returned with reinforcement. "I'm gonna make you leave," she said, holding up a loaded handgun.

This wasn't the first time Mom had pulled a gun on a family member. That time Walter had been the target after one of their arguments, when both of them escalated into madness. She gave him scratches and bruises; he gave her a black eye and a bloody lip. That evening she wielded the same gun and issued a warning, "You better sleep with one eye open, Bastard! I'll kill you if you ever hit me again!" Mom could provoke more than anyone I'd ever seen. Still, Walter was a jackass for hitting her. No woman deserves to be hit, and outside of a life-or-death situation, no one should be threatened with a gun.

Her reaction was too harsh for Tom's mistake, too. I believe, at some point, any rational person can snap under too much pressure, too much pain. This was no cartoon, where the coyote survives the fall off the rocky bluff. This was real life; where there were consequences, real blood, and heartache.

Mom continued the verbal assault on Tom, "I mean it. Get out!" The gun tucked by her side.

"I'm just making a friggin' sandwich!" Tom said. He slammed down the loaf of bread and bologna, and the butter knife fell to the tile floor.

He surrendered, rushing outside, where he screamed, kicked my truck, and pulled plants from the ground and planter boxes.

Mom finally reached the police. I wished she hadn't.

Knowing the cops were on their way, Tom finally broke, his yelling turned to sobbing. It wasn't the first time the police had been called to our family home, and it probably wouldn't be the last. I felt sorry for Tom, for us, for this. This isn't the way it's supposed to be.

But maybe apart from each other was best, where we could no longer harm one another.

In the heat of my Seattle apartment, Tom, Walter, Mom, and I unpacked the boxes that had traveled more than sixteen hundred miles. My mom, too, had moved out of her mother's house at a young age. She'd grown up as an only child under strict parents on the south side of Chicago. She adored her dad, Tommy, but he'd broken her trust in her teenage years when Grandma made her spy on him with his mistress. He died of a heart attack when Mom was eighteen. After high school, without any money, Mom's dream of becoming a biochemist or going to art school had dead-ended. She could only mourn her losses and paint her tears into an oil portrait of her dad. Grandma, who loved live band lounges, late night TV mysteries, and the Pope, had been disciplining Mom through childhood with chastisements like, "Keep your dirty hands off my French Provincial furniture." She finally drove Mom out the house at age twenty and into the arms of my handsome, Iowa-born father, Kenny, who was three years older. I'd found a letter in Mom's scrapbook addressed to Grandma, as plain as "Gone fishin'," it read:

> *Mom,*
> *Kenny and I got married yesterday at 1:30 in Evanston in a chapel. I love him very much. Try to understand if it's at all possible. We're going to Aunt Irene's. You can call us there if you want to.*
>
> *Love, your daughter.*

Mom was like a beautiful butterfly held too long in a confined cocoon. She needed to flitter and fly and sprinkle her glitter all over, but by the time Mom was my age, she was already married with a two-year-old, me.

Now here I was in the same position my mom had been in. As much as I wanted family in my life, I'd moved to Seattle to get away.

"You've always been independent," Mom said, on the verge of crying. "You've pushed me away since birth. You never wanted to be held too tight." Perhaps even as a baby I could sense life's chaos, or more likely I was just allergic to breast milk.

My first vivid memory came during potty training in Cicero, a suburb of West Chicago. Mom towered above my tiny self and asked, "You don't want to be my age wearing a diaper, do you?" I felt pressure, like I had to choose right then. A big person? Wearing a diaper? No, I don't want that. That's just weird. I better get this down. Today. I don't know if I mastered it that day or within months, but it was my first step on the road to independence—dumping the diaper. Though, Mom says it started fresh out of the womb.

A few years later, as a preschooler, I pulled my big-wheeled, wire cart to the corner grocery store, modeling the elderly Italian and Polish ladies in the neighborhood and admiring the babushkas tied around their heads. I skipped to the store, snapping my fingers and repeating the ditty, "A loaf of bread, a container of milk, a stick of butter," like that cool cartoon girl on *Sesame Street*. In the back of my mind, I also sprinkled in the mantra Mom taught me in case any weirdos messed with me along the way, "Kick him in the nuts. Kick him in the nuts." The instructions were clear. "Aim hard between the legs, but don't ever do it to your brother. Ever." She said to always yell, scream, and fight back if anyone made me uncomfortable or touched me inappropriately. "Listen to your instincts. Be like a wild animal," she said. "Go for the jugular." I had this part down.

Now in my Seattle apartment, I placed photo albums and chotchkies in milk crate bookshelves. "Are you sure you want to do this?" Mom asked. "We can pack it all up and drive it back home."

The truth was, I wasn't sure. Maybe my breaking free was born of necessity—survival—not desire. I'd wished for stability since I was a kid. To stay in one town, in one school district, with one whole family. I was the "new kid" five times by the time I was in sixth grade, a total of seven by the time we moved to Missouri just before my senior year of high school, where I ran out of school years. I wanted to call one place *home*. And I had chosen Seattle.

I simply said, "I don't want to go back."

As I unpacked another box, the volatile scent and signature squeak of the magic marker against packing tape evoked memories of the many childhood moves, a life in motion.

Through my preschool years, we lived in a downstairs apartment near Sportsman's race track. The track was founded by Al Capone as a dog racing track in 1928, but I only saw thoroughbreds there and Tony the Italian selling the best Chicago dogs from his stand out front. Cicero, spotlighted during the Chicago Freedom Movement of 1966, was sadly known at the time for racial hatred. Derogatory slurs were tossed around the neighborhood about every ethnicity: Spics, Micks, Dagos, Japs, Gooks, Chinks, and us, the Polacks, the butt of all the funniest jokes. Mom said it was wrong, "No one should ever use those names."

When I'd point to people and ask Grandma things like "Why are those black men wearing pink spongey curlers in their hair like you do?" She'd just tug my arm hard and "shush" me instead of telling me why. Mom told us, straight-up, "To loosen tight, curly hair you use bigger rollers."

Mom could talk to anyone. She didn't fear different types of people. "You don't have to be afraid of strangers," she said. "Look them in the eye. Shake their hand. Say, 'It's nice to meet you.' You just have to beware of the occasional weirdo. Honey, weirdos come in all ages, shapes, and colors."

At home, we mostly listened to Motown and danced in the living room to *Soul Train* instead of *American Bandstand*. I liked the way they danced on TV, though Mom said the best dancers were deaf, because they *felt* the music in their bones. People different from me. Deaf people. People who limped or talked funny. People from other towns, other countries, with different language, food, and culture interested me. If you were different, I wanted to know about you.

My mom's grandfather, great-grandpa Joe from Poland, or Pa as we all called him, was living with us. I remember him as a giant man with big hands and a funny accent. He was eighteen when he left behind his family in Poland and toted himself and his sixteen-year-old brother Andy to the US. Pa became a butcher and married young. His wife, Maryann, died at age thirty-six, when my grandma was only thirteen. He raised his two teenage daughters, my grandma, Felicia, and her sister, Irene. When his brother got killed in a bar fight, he cared for his brother's kids, too. His second marriage to Anna didn't last, but his Catholic faith didn't allow for divorce. He stayed married, but bounced between Grandma's, Aunt Irene's, and our apartment.

As a young widow, Grandma started dating again, and so did my mom, who was in her late teens. But Pa didn't allow other men around. He'd wait up late at night for Grandma to come home and threaten her with his big fist. Then Pa had to live with his other daughter, my great Aunt Irene. She and Grandma told childhood stories about how Pa punished them with a leather razor strap, the same one Mom used on my brother and me. It was handed down like some honored family heirloom. My grandma and her sister would lock themselves in the bathroom and sleep in the bathtub all night to keep away from him. He yelled at them a lot, even as adults, which was why he had to live with us for a while—they needed a break.

He'd sit on the front stoop and peel an apple in one long spiral with his pocketknife, which is cool when you're a kid. He held our tiny hands and took us on the bus to the local kiddie pool or the park. He read us lots of stories in his Polish accent. We loved him living with us, but then one day Pa was gone from our home. Afraid he'd stumble and fall on us kids from drinking too much, Mom and Dad insisted he moved back in with Aunt Irene. The grandpa shuffle continued.

Pa was good to my brother and me. Sadly, years later he died of gangrene in his bad foot. He was the first to go in my life besides my first goldfishes, Jack and Jill. Mom told us she gave Jack and Jill to Santa for kids who didn't have any presents, but I knew they went down the toilet and up into heaven. Now they were with mom's dad and Great-grandpa Joe.

I worried as a kid. I needed to learn to take care of myself, because people might not be there for you when you need them. I lost significant people in my life before I lost all my baby teeth. People you loved went away. They died. Or some just wanted to die.

Sometimes we just moved.

I hoped to avoid writing "Laura's stuff" on another cardboard box for a long time. I asked Mom, "Why did we move so much and have to go to all those different schools?"

"I had to go where I could find work," she replied.

It seemed I was following in Mom's footsteps. Despite wanting to sink my roots down deep into terra firma, like a colossal Midwestern oak tree, the wind was sailing me toward the distant Bering Sea in search of a paycheck. This time I would pack a sole duffel bag with a baggage tag instead of a cardboard box inscribed with magic marker.

6

TRAINING

"ARE you here for the shoe sale, too?" Those were the first words
Stephanie spoke to me, as we met for the first time in the sprawl-
ing parking lot for day one of training at the National Oceanic
and Atmospheric Association in Seattle. With that one sentence,
all the loneliness and blows of rejection that had built up during
my nine-month struggle in this new city was cushioned instantly
by a friend. Stef was the patch over the hole in my sinking boat,
and I didn't realize how large it was until I stopped bailing. She
was witty and good-natured, packed with energy and a positive
attitude. Her blue, deep-set eyes beneath heavy brows, severe
when unsmiling, easily teared up from laughter. A fellow Midwesterner, she wasn't afraid of hard work or talking to strangers,
and we had a shared appreciation for Chicago-style pizza, cheese
curds, and Friday night fish fries.

She was a welcomed relief from the organic veggie-obsessed
Seattleites I encountered waitressing. They'd rattle off their litany
of questions about food: What's on it? What's in it? Where was it
grown, and were any feelings hurt in the process? In the Midwest,

there were a lot fewer questions, "Are you hungry? It's a hot dog. Shut up and eat."

We related on many levels, and when I noticed we were the same height, too, I asked her, "What size shoes do you wear?" she put one foot down to match mine and said, "Size Clydesdale." I knew in that moment we'd be great friends.

We entered a classroom of two dozen students with one thing in common: we were science folks in transition who couldn't find "real" jobs and couldn't stand the thought of working at the wrong one. As I scanned my classmates, another childhood ditty hummed in my mind, "One of these things is not like the other . . . One of these things doesn't belong." That "thing" was me. Perhaps I wasn't as much of a tomboy as I'd once thought. They say when we get away from the familiar, we become most like ourselves. Who would I become after three months on a ship and totally disconnected from everything, and everyone, that I knew?

My job would be to estimate the size of the haul, sample the catch, record the data, and once a week relay it back to NMFS in Seattle via COMSAT (Communications Satellite Corporation), a precursor to email. A thin, soft-spoken woman taught the class as if from a victim's perspective. She stood in front of us, slouched over in a muted yellow button-down blouse—nothing like I expected from a teacher and mentor. She had been an observer years earlier, but I couldn't picture her making it through a full day at sea handling fish.

"Your time at sea will be the most trying three months of your life," she began with a sigh. "For the females in the class, of course we try to prevent sexual harassment, but it can be an issue in a male-dominated environment."

Stephanie tilted her head towards me and raised her eyebrows. I knew we were thinking the same thing: Who would harass whom? We both had brothers and preferred to hang out with guys and do "guy" stuff. I couldn't imagine sexual harassment happening to either of us, but I could picture Stef or me resisting the urge to plant a football player fanny-slap on one of our crewmates.

The instructor continued for the telltale bonus round. "The waves will be rough. You won't sleep much, and you'll likely be seasick."

"She's teasing us," I whispered to Stef, trying to downplay the challenges we'd likely encounter up there.

"Sign me up," said Stef smiling behind her cupped hand. Our similar styles of humor notched us up a level on the friendship scale. Humor would be necessary to get us through class and the months to follow.

The instructor outlined some of our duties: "For a special project, you'll collect cod stomach contents, otoliths (ear bones), or salmon scales. And if you're lucky enough to drag up a dead sea lion, you'll have to hack its snout off to recover the teeth for aging purposes."

How many people outside of doctors, butchers, or serial killers had experience sawing off body parts? I had. During my veterinary assistant job I helped amputate that pug's mangled leg with a Gigli saw, a flexible wire, like a guitar string lined with tiny razors. That pug was my demise and the end of that dream. Now as the instructor described what I'd need to do, I began to see the worth of my various past work experiences.

For weeks we listened to the dramatic warnings: we'd work long hours on a frozen ice rink of a metal deck or in a subzero processing factory. Our fingers and toes would turn to popsicles, and if we did go overboard, we'd likely die even with our survival suits on. Stef and I downplayed the scare tactics and convinced ourselves she was exaggerating until we saw the training videos. Filmed during real-life situations, the footage depicted raging seas, ice-covered equipment, crews darting across slippery decks to dodge waves and swinging cables, and mega-tons of fish to sample. Near the end of the video, in the dark classroom, Stef gave me a single raised eyebrow and said, "Maybe it'll be scarier than we think." On the front cover of my manual I made a note: "WORRY MORE!"

Worry is something I had down. Worried about choosing wrong. Worried about the welfare of my family left in my wake. Worried I wasn't good enough or smart enough. Worried about being on the wrong path. But I was determined that now, instead of being voted "The Cutest" as in high school, I would be known as "The Girl Most Likely to Man Up and Go Work on Fishing Boats in Alaska."

During my final weeks ashore, I called friends and family strewn across the US hoping to hear affirmation. But no one was prepared to hear that I was flying to Alaska to work on a fishing vessel alongside rugged men and slimy fish amidst severe weather.

The questions were the same: "What kind of boat will you be on? How long will you be out there?"

"I don't know yet," I responded. "My vessel could be 40 to 400 feet long, and each trip could last from two days to two months straight. I could be on multiple boats."

I waited for encouraging words, but instead I heard only, "I'd never do such a thing!" and "That's nuts!" and "Are you sure?"

No, I'm not sure, I thought.

When I was in college, I'd scuba dived with manatees, sharks, and electric eels; repelled off cliffs; Eskimo rolled kayaks; gone spelunking in Ozark caves between stalactites and hordes of dive-bombing bats; canoed swift creeks and hiked alone to high mountain peaks. This would be a very different kind of adventure.

My mom, who avoided driving a winter mile without a twenty-pound bag of salt, a shovel, and a snowmobile suit in the trunk, was not thrilled about my Alaskan excursion.

"Laura, those guys are different and you are not the typical woman encountered up there. Rain gear and boots cannot hide what you've got. Believe me, you're not what they're expecting. Be careful."

"Mom. I can handle it. I'll be fine." I wanted some encouragement from her, but only heard "What ifs?" Maybe she'd always been fearful, but appeared unwavering to my younger self. Now it fell to me to be the strong one.

She asked, "Aren't you . . . afraid?"

I considered my mom's life, a journey I respected but hoped not to repeat. I didn't want that kind of struggle. "Not really, Mom. I'm more scared of being a waitress with a biology degree for the rest of my life." It was an honest answer.

I was the first in my lineage to attend college. In my family, you built yourself from the ground up, even without a firm foundation, or direction, or assurances, like "You can always rely on us."

No one had been there for Mom either. Her waitressing and bartending paid the bills during my early childhood. She'd often say, "I don't care if I have to work three jobs. I refuse to be some welfare queen." She wanted to better our lives and never passed blame or made excuses. I admired her fortitude and carried that spirit with me. I had an obsessive desire to be in a fulfilling career and provide for myself, alone, before love and marriage, before life could be "right" in my eyes.

By the time I was in kindergarten we had migrated north from street-tough Cicero to laid back Lake Villa, near the Wisconsin border. Dad found sporadic construction or painting jobs, and in the winter he plowed snow from the neighbors' driveways for cash. Mom, who had been raised in Chicago, described Dad's rural Iowa upbringing as poor and pathetic. He'd served in the Navy before he met and married Mom. She wanted to show him a different side of life, one wide open with opportunities.

In Lake Villa, we lived in a quaint house with attic bedrooms and a raised hump in the middle of the living room floor, where the kerosene heater was perched, glowing like a lighthouse on cold nights. Our quarter acre abutted a swamp filled with cattails that some kids burned to the ground for fun on Halloween each year. We lived in the burbs more than an hour away from Grandma, who didn't understand why we moved to the "boonies."

Mom usually encouraged us to roam and explore in the wetland marsh and ride our bikes through the neighborhood; other times we were told to "go play in traffic."

A giant weeping willow stood tall in our backyard, casting a shadow on Mom's lifeless convertible, the centerpiece of one of our favorite games. With four flat tires sinking into the mud, it had little hope of ever seeing the pavement again. Still, she couldn't give it up; it was the promise of a shinier future ahead—her behind the wheel, carefree, with the wind blowing through her hair. My brother and I took turns "driving" the jalopy. I'd wrap a scarf around my head like a Hollywood star. Tom would push in the dashboard lighter and light the stick protruding out my lips like a real gentleman would. We played out all the places we could go in the car: down a country road, between the skyscrapers of downtown Chicago, in races and demolition derbies, or on a highway to somewhere far away.

Usually, my brother and I gravitated toward playing with the earth: kicking stones; whacking sticks; holding snakes, frogs, baby bunnies, and slider turtles hostage in a shoe box for show-and-tell; and running through the rain or snow with mouths wide open. Did we choose these activities or did they choose us? If we spent too much time in the house, Mom would say, "It's a beautiful day out there. Why am I looking at you right now? Go outside. Don't come back in until I ring the dinner bell or it's dark."

We sometimes dressed in hand-me-downs, the Salvation Army brought us toys some years, and we stretched one gallon of milk into two by mixing it with powdered, but we didn't feel deprived. Mom would say, "Let's go slummin'," and we'd head to the thrift stores in search of steals and treasures. Every Christmas Mom reminded us, "We need to give some things away to the poor kids who don't have anything." She always made Christmas special, hanging doll clothes on the tree for me and giving my brother a special truck or model car he really wanted. And she artfully decorated our Easter baskets and filled them with high-quality candy from a fancy chocolate store. We were lucky. We were spoiled. We had too much. Some kids didn't even have food.

Mom was the bold centerpiece in our lives. Dad—six-foot-four and the handsomest man in the world besides Elvis—was present, but next to her he faded into the background, a face in a washed-out photo. Dad sometimes took Tom and me to his jobs, where he dressed in white carpenter pants and a white crew neck with a pack of Camels or Lucky Strikes rolled up in his short sleeve. His name was tattooed in muddy green ink on his bicep. His sun-kissed pompadour, bronzed skin, and wristwatch were usually speckled with paint.

His toolbox was a source of play. I'd write prices on the wood with his big flat pencil and play hardware store. Sometimes I'd hammer nails, snap the blue chalk line, or paint a section of the wall with him. He'd say, "Phillips," "Flathead," or "Wrench," and I'd grab the tools like a surgeon's assistant. Mom wanted him to try harder and find more work, more pay. Anything steady rather than spurts and stops. Dad barely had a plan for tomorrow, let alone a road map for our compact family's future.

Mom worked nights as a bartender, which was probably why she started to sleep so much during the day with the shades drawn and a pillow over her head. Dad stayed home at night to tend to us kids and read us bedtime stories. They'd sometimes fight when they thought we were asleep. Whenever we'd sneak downstairs from our attic bedrooms, they'd yell, "Go back to bed! Everything is okay." It didn't sound like everything was okay. I didn't know why they argued so much, but Mom said he fueled his jealous thoughts about her whereabouts with a nightly six-pack of Old Style. Dad liked his beer and would crush the empty cans with his bare hands. He also folded over the six plastic rings into one circle and ripped it wide open. He said the plastic rings could get entangled around a bird's head or maybe even a sea turtle swimming far away in the ocean.

I loved Daddy for caring about the sea turtles and birds, and us kids. Tall and strong, he could fix just about anything. He built us a sandbox, where I'd sit and pick ants from a drooping peony blossom; a swing where I sang and soared into the clouds like a bird; and a playhouse the size of a tool shed. He painted the wood happy colors: sunshine yellow, spring green, and sherbet orange.

One night while Mom was working and my brother and I slept upstairs, the house filled with black smoke and smelled like burning plastic. Dad ran into our rooms. He swooped us both up, clad in our polyester footie pajamas, and carried us outside to his truck. We could hear the echo of the fire engine sirens as they sped our way. Dad had fallen asleep on the overstuffed, orange-brown couch with a lit cigarette. The house was spared, but the couch burned faster than the cattails in the swamp on Halloween. Soon after that the bank took Dad's truck, and then without any warning he was gone. Then a nice Greek lady stayed with us through the night sometimes. I told my brother that Dad was probably out looking for more work.

And then we moved again.

Our little family was always in transition. And I was carrying on the tradition, working temporary jobs to get the bills paid while waiting for the next opportunity. As a freshly trained fisheries observer, now my work would begin.

7

STANDING TALL IN MAN BOOTS

CRUNCH! Scrape! The sound of something battering against the hull startled me awake in my dark bunk. I broke free from my flannel-lined cocoon and threw on my oversized sweatshirt and baggy sweatpants, shoved my long ponytail through the back of a baseball cap, and sprang up to the bridge. There, with eyes still half shut, I looked out the expansive windows. "What the . . .?" I asked Captain Gabe while grabbing his arm like a vice grip. "You're kidding me!"

"Don't worry," Captain Gabe said, grinning from ear to ear. "This amount of ice is normal in these parts for April."

"What? No one warned me about ice!" Great. The saltwater, at twenty-seven degrees Fahrenheit, fluctuates between ice water and actual ice. Images of the Titanic came to mind.

"We can get out and walk on it like polar bears if you want," he offered.

We couldn't. I wouldn't.

We'd been steaming for more than eighteen hours and were now about equidistant between Russia and Alaska's Aleutian Islands. The outside temperature read twenty degrees Fahrenheit, but the wind chill registered subzero. From winter into spring, the ice floe melts and recedes further north with each passing month. We would fish the southern edge of the ice along shallow continental shelves and the productive thermocline, where warmer water meets cooler water. Here, in this mixing zone, the lower salinity of melting ice influences phytoplankton productivity and typically provides excellent fishing grounds for our target species, rockfish and Pacific cod. Our fishing gear had already been set.

Over the following weeks, we'd steadily carve our way through massive, six-inch-thick sheets of ice. We wouldn't venture too much farther north, where the ice pack could be a couple of yards thick. It was incredible to be fishing in a region between Alaska and Siberia that was part of the Bering Land Bridge, once dry land before the last ice age ended more than 11,000 years ago. As the continental ice sheets melted, much of the world's freshwater was released, raising sea levels to cover the land where we were fishing. We were north of The Pribilof Islands, the only visible land masses in the Bering Sea remaining from the central Land Bridge.

Hundreds of white, van-sized puzzle pieces floated around us, crushed and dispersed by the ship's bow. The frigid wind grabbed the ocean spray and layer upon layer coated the gear, crane, railings, and deck, turning them into ice sculptures. The crew would soon be sent out with baseball bats and hefty rubber mallets to pound away at the shiny frozen slabs and icicles, caving them to the deck, and then launching or shoveling them overboard. Beyond the 180-degree panel of windows, I saw nothing but ocean and sky. We had carved a dark blue band of navigable wake through a white blanket that now zippered shut behind us—a path of no return. I'd heard about boats freezing over, but I never expected to be plowing through endless rinks of ice like a massive waterborne Zamboni.

After two days of travel with neither land nor boat in sight, my holiday on the Bering Sea was over. Now the work would begin. Despite the weeks of training, I felt completely inadequate in the job before me. I stared into the dark those first two nights aboard, recalling tidbits of wisdom I'd learned through lectures, videos, manuals, logbooks, and word of mouth. The guts, gore, and scare tactics of the classroom stuck with me like a horror film. Still, I woke to a true-life nightmare: acronyms to decipher, data to crunch and extrapolate, and abstract scenarios whirling around me like evil spirits. The calculus, trigonometry, and geometry I studied in college hadn't prepared me for this job that was a giant, looming word problem. Math. Math was my new reality. Oh, and ice.

The captain and crew had spent two hours setting nearly ten miles of nine-millimeter nylon groundline suspending approximately 15,000 hooks across the sea floor between two anchors. Each set would "soak" for about three hours, waiting for the fish to bite before we'd haul back the catch. Retrieval of the entire line could take seven to nine hours, depending on the substrate, weather, currents, and the amount of fish coming aboard. Floating buoys and javelin-like, aluminum poles with diamond-shaped reflector flags marked the anchors' positions, which was recorded on an electronic plotter and located by radar. The captain worried we could easily lose our gear if the wind shifted and the ice dragged our buoys away. I waited on tiptoe behind Captain Gabe at the helm to watch my first haulback—my first catch on the Bering Sea.

Russell, the crewman who had traded my gear for his box of lettuce, stood starboard on deck. The crew called him Rico Suave. Other than his blue eyes ringed in onyx halos looking out from beneath his hood, I hadn't noticed much about him then. But now

I could track him with my eyes closed. As far as I could tell, he was the only one aboard who wore cologne. *Obsession*. It lured me in like a freshly baited hook. Of Native and Black American decent, Russell was over six feet tall, broad but lean, with freckled, café mocha skin. He wore his hair tightly clipped into a fade and a well-groomed beard and mustache. On the bow, Russell pointed to the buoy marker and then heaved a grapple thirty feet out and over the buoy line, like he was roping a steer. I was impressed.

Captain Gabe shouted, "Righteous! Nailed it!" While I was thinking, "Giddyup, cowboy."

Russell hauled in the buoy, the aluminum pole flag with attached radar detector, and the thirty-pound lead weight that kept it upright as it bobbed in the waves. He flipped the line below deck through the factory hatch to Dean, puffing away on his cigarette.

"Got it," Dean shouted as he grabbed the line from Russell and connected it to the offshore hauler, or power block. As we moved toward the line, the hauler mechanically pulled in the line. The anchor and line had been uprooted, along with my life, and were now in the hands of the captain and these fishermen. Though the gear was secured to the seafloor for a time, the vessel, and thus we, would always be in motion, against wind, waves, currents, and one other.

Russell easily slung the anchor, a fifty-pound hunk of steel, over his sculpted shoulders. I thought, *that* could sell jeans. My eyes were left wanting to see more. I'd eagerly be back for the next haul . . . and the next. I wanted to be unaffected, but the sight and smell of this man made me weak.

Outside, seawater illuminated the edges of the ice chunks bobbing in the ocean like slush in a snow cone. I'd never witnessed such wild ocean that seemed to go on forever. That's was when I realized that sport fishing, as much as I loved it, for me was less about catching fish and more about it taking me to beautiful places—lakes, streams, and oceans—where I could find a little peace. I hung halfway out the window behind the captain, only popping back in to defrost my numbing face and Rudolph nose. As each ice chunk broke and sloshed against the side of the boat, I waited impatiently to see my first fish come up on the longline. Incredible to think that this is where much of our seafood came from.

Hordes of gulls, with their boomerang wings, soared level with the wheelhouse window as if they were tracking my every move. I'd been somewhat timid of birds since second grade when I was assaulted by a rogue crow in Chicago on my walk to school. It swooped down from the city sky and clawed at my long hair. It only stopped when I struck it with my metal lunchbox. Now, all these birds dive-bombing around me freaked me out a bit.

"Gabe, they're kinda scary," I said. "I mean, they're *really* looking at me."

"Dude, they're just wondering how they can eat out your eyeballs," he remarked, and then explained how gulls always go for the eyes of a carcass first. I imagined my bloated corpse floating behind the boat with several seagulls perched on my head slurping my eyes out like oysters on the half shell. They'd probably pull my hair out, too, like that savage crow in Chicago.

The vessel slowly moved toward the gear to lift it up and avoid dragging it across the seafloor. The gear came up in units called "skates." One set of line contained up to seventy-five skates. We fished 200 to 400 meters deep, where Pacific cod and rockfish habitat overlapped, so I expected to see both. The elongated, fat-bellied Pacific cod would be a cinch to identify with barbels on their chins like candlewick goatees, but the variety of rockfish would be a bigger challenge.

"Come on. Come on!" Captain Gabe said, drumming the steering column. The first few hooks came up bare. He hoped for a good catch; his ego and the crew's paychecks rested on it.

I recalled early mornings before college classes spent with my boyfriend on Table Rock Lake in Missouri, speeding up to forty mph in a bass boat with my eyes peeled back from the wind in search of fish popping to the surface. I loved to fish; there is faith in fishing, to be persistent, to keep trying, to hope for a bite. But I also wanted to be at his side, hear him call me "Sweetie," and kiss in between long casts. The challenge in fishing laid in determining the best depth and habitat for the time of day and season. Large-mouth, smallmouth, or Kentucky bass? Where were the big lunkers now? Were they biting on Point Nine? Were they hiding in the submerged logs, where we might lose our gear, or under the floating racks of wood and debris? Should we jig deep or flick our wrists to work a top-water bait like a Zara spook? A fish on the line was instant reward. The bigger, the better. The more you caught, the more you bragged, and the brighter your day.

Seconds later, from outside the wheelhouse we heard, "Fish on!" from Dean, leaning out the factory hatch below us, looking up at me with his green eyes.

"Money!" shouted Gabe, with a pump of his fists; you could feel the surge of testosterone.

Huge, thick-lipped fish broke the surface chop every four to five feet, dangling from circle hooks and twelve-inch leaders, or gangions, like spinning pendants. Certain they were Pacific cod-fish, or P-cod, I was overjoyed.

I observed the first third of the haul to learn the process, review the species I might encounter, and shake off my rawness before I officially began sampling. Another line had been set parallel a half-mile away. Dean, positioned at the bulwark roller, a spinning horizontal steel rod that supports tension of the incoming line and the point at which the fish are removed from their hooks. There he stood at the hatch only several feet above the ocean's surface, controlling the speed of the approaching line. As the fish came up he stabbed each one in the head with a long, sharp metal hook called a gaff. He tugged them off their hooks as they came over the roller and before they hit another pair of metal rollers, smaller and positioned vertically, called the fish stripper, aptly nicknamed the crucifier. This whole process seemed as bad as my bonking spawned-out research salmon over the head, except these fish had a lot more life left to them.

"Ahh, damn it! Get it, get it. *Get* it," Dean yelped as he failed to bring in a fat cod that had dropped off the line.

Another deckhand, Larone, a tall, soft-middled, self-deprecating guy with a frayed afro, stood by Dean's side at the roller. Cool, quiet, and mysterious with slow, deliberate speech, Larone was an expert quick draw with a pole gaff. He swiftly snatched the fallen fish before it could be swept away on the waves. If either of the two deckhands missed too many fish, they were temporarily replaced, like a benched first stringer in basketball, with someone who was more fresh. You had to earn the golden positions and higher pay at the hatch.

Watching them work with the hooks, fast-moving line, powerful motors, and the surrounding ice water, my worry kicked in. What if a hook caught Dean's hand and jammed it between the crucifier? Larone could slip and ram a gaff through his arm. We were at least eighteen hours from a hospital. What if either of them leaned out too far to grab a fish and was tossed into the frigid waves? Beneath their rain gear they wore only fleece Stormy Seas jackets with the built-in flotation, which might be enough to retrieve the dead body.

As I watched this mysterious new life before me, the mixed bag of past jobs that led me to seek a career in science rapid-fired in my mind. Weekends in college spent at the fish hatchery suctioning morts (dead fish) out of fry tanks, jackknifing the feed truck while attempting to fill it at the silo, and cleaning urinals and buffing floors at the visitor's center. Internships included a summer in Nags Head at the North Carolina Aquarium, educating visitors about ocean life, and sampling juvenile finfish in Pamlico Sound with the Department of Natural Resources. Another summer, I scored a research fellowship in my college's organic chemistry lab synthesizing floral-scented compounds. Senior year awarded me with a summer research fellowship at Mount Desert Island Biological Laboratory in Bar Harbor, Maine. I wondered then how lancing and squeezing marine bloodworms to study osmoregulation (maintaining the balance of salts in cell fluids) would look on a résumé to a future employer. All these experiences paved my way to the Bering Sea, but deep down I wasn't yet sure I made the right decision to take on the fisheries observer position, thinking I'd probably miss out on "real" job opportunities on land.

As James Brown's "Get Up Offa That Thing" blasted through the wheelhouse speakers, I watched the fish come aboard, one by one. I knew cod, but worried about the unknown bycatch. Bycatch are fish unintended for capture, but are incidentally caught and discarded because of low economic value, or fishing regulations require their release. Would there be many species, and would I have to use the dichotomous key to identify them? Class and lessons learned were increasingly distant.

Next, two- to three-foot-long, dark brown, rhomboidal saucers with wings and narrow tails came up between cod. Skates! Then, suddenly, Dean slowed the line. What did he see approaching? It was flat and a dark brown to olive color. It surfaced like a thick, meaty surfboard, dense and elongate, white underneath. Got it: a Pacific halibut, the largest of all flatfish. Flatfish are unusual in that they begin with one eye on each side of their body like a regularly shaped fish, but as they develop, one eye migrates to meet the other as the fish begins to swim on its side. Each flatfish species is generally either left-eyed or right-eyed, like the halibut.

With many of them being longer than my five-feet-ten frame, it was unfeasible to bring halibut aboard to measure and weigh like smaller bycatch. Instead, I hung out the window and assessed their lengths against premeasured increments marked on the outside of the vessel. Weights were later estimated using a predetermined average length-to-weight table created specifically for halibut.

"That halibut is h*uuu*ge!" I said, peering down alongside the vessel to see the whole fish. "It's over six feet long. That sucker is like, what, 400 pounds?" Male halibut rarely grew more than three feet long, but females could reach eight feet long and weigh over 500 pounds.

Captain Gabe wrinkled up his face. "Naaa. Look at it. It's tiny. It's a baby!" he said, trying to convince me I had exaggerated its size. Small halibut were nicknamed "chickens," but none we encountered were poultry sized.

Halibut counted as bycatch under an economically valuable category called prohibs, or prohibited species. NMFS assigns stringent catch limits on them and forbids their retention unless licensed to do so. Salmon and herring, along with opilio, tanner, and king crabs, though we wouldn't see many, were also considered prohibs. The total weight of prohibs, including each pound of halibut, counted against the vessel's limited proportion of bycatch and the total tonnage allotted for the entire fleet. It was no wonder Captain Gabe downplayed the length. It was my word against his, but my data and reports had to be accurate, no matter how he tried to influence my estimates with his dimples.

Dean slid his gaff around the circle hook to shake off the mammoth, minimally tearing its thin, tensile lips before it reached the rollers or crucifier. Fatigued with minor injury, but alive and intact, the halibut soared back into the deep like a weighted door.

I raved about the majesty of the halibut, while Captain Gabe ranted about his competitors.

"Laura, some of these companies fish damn dirty," he said. "They don't give a shit if they haul in tons of bycatch as long as their boats come back full of product."

"What do you do if you're rolling in tons of halibut?" I asked.

"Move my ass somewhere else, where they're not as thick!" he said, scowling. I had exposed a nerve.

"And if the boat doesn't move?" I asked, unaware of the industry's politics.

"If vessels fish dirty and cause the premature shutdown of a fishery, word spreads fast throughout the fleet. They become pariahs," he explained. "But, ultimately, we all suffer and go home with empty pockets." I still had a lot to learn.

My sampling would be split between the wheelhouse and the factory. From the wheelhouse, I sub-sampled at least one-third of the entire haul to determine catch composition. For two hours, I hung my head out the window to watch over the line entering the factory, long enough to lose feeling in my face. Fish after fish, my fingers juggled several tally counters, one per abundant species. Other incidentals were tallied with a pencil on a white plastic deck board. I would later transfer all my figures to paper data sheets and send my weekly totals in by COMSAT. Each entry would be examined for errors when I returned to Seattle for debriefing months later.

From his cozy chair, Captain Gabe reminded me, "Okay, Observer Girl, the easy part is over. It's time for you to get sampling in the factory." It was time to enter deep into the belly of the whale.

I quickly learned that a "standard" processing factory did not exist. Each boat, deck, wheelhouse, factory, and, thus, an observer's sampling station was configured differently. Despite a hand sketch of the vessel's layout in a logbook during training and a brief look during my initial tour of the vessel, I was headed into the working factory blind.

Now I had to gear up at the entrance, away from the warmth of the wheelhouse.

"Can't is not a word!" My mom's voice ringing out from my childhood. "God helps those who help themselves!"

With no teacher to guide me, fellow observer to ask, or computer on which to google "How to be a fisheries observer," I was spurred on by Mom's words. I also remembered those I'd written on the front of my training manual: WORRY MORE! Would I remember what to do? It was time to find out, so I throttled forward into the factory. Solo.

It was time to suit up, suck it up, and find out. Under my orange Grundén raincoat I layered long underwear, sweatpants, a turtleneck, and a hooded sweatshirt. A wool hat was pulled down tight. I stuffed my feet into thick, wooly liners and XtraTuf boots. Rubber bands held the wide-legged overalls tight to my ankles.

My man boots would be indestructible, like Wonder Woman's wrist cuffs, holding me up straight against sloshing saltwater, powerful wind, and anything else I might need to step in, over or through.

My hands, enlarged by black wool liners and waterproof gloves, made me think of Polish Pa and his big hands that always seemed to be waving at someone. If he could see me now, he'd probably throw up his bear paws and yell, "Women should look like women!" and come after me, swinging the two flapping tongues of the leather razor strap, his favorite instrument of discipline.

My brother and I used to play ball, running bases, and Ghost in the Graveyard or flashlight tag in the streets of my great aunt's Chicago neighborhood with a girl named Sue. She was one of the *Bad News Bear* types. She loved sports, had a pixie haircut, and wore sneakers and baseball caps—a real tomboy. If Pa saw her within steps of the front porch or close to the house, he'd throw up his arms and chase after her like a lunatic. Without his dentures, he'd shout in his old-world accent, "Summ-omm-bitch, I k*iii*ll you! No boys in this house!" She was a girl. A fun, cool girl. He didn't like her in "boy clothes." I'm sure he wouldn't approve of mine right now.

I drank in an extra deep breath and took my first working pass through the processing factory. To my surprise, fresh fish and men covered in fish didn't smell that bad. The men sorted and packed the cod into metal trays but held my gaze with laser focus. Perhaps my mom was right when she warned, "Rain gear and boots can't hide what you've got." But to me, wearing foul weather gear was like slipping into a Bering Sea burka, shrink wrapping my pheromones, shielding me from storms, fish slime, my femaleness, the men's eyes, my own insecurities, and Grandpa Joe, in case he was watching me from Heaven.

I walked past Josef, the thin, boyish Czech with the sweet face and two ponytails standing erect on top of his head, like a freshly groomed Shih Tzu puppy. Like me he was a newbie, an easy target. The guys were hard on new crewmen, especially those labeled as slackers or fakers, pretending to be ill or injured. On a fishing boat, if a crewman had a temperature less than 104 degrees and was conscious, didn't have a limb visibly bent in the wrong direction, something swollen to twice the normal size, or a deep, blood-gushing wound, he was probably slacking or faking. In junior high, he would have gotten a wedgie or been shoved into an empty locker, but on a fishing boat he'd be teased mercilessly, ridiculed, or might discover that someone had urinated all over his bunk mattress. No amount of punishment or harassment was off limits. The guys poked fun at Josef's floppy hairstyle, a cultural norm in his country. Despite his hard work, on this boat he was a tender little girl in pigtails. I wanted to shout, "It's *just hair*," but I was outnumbered, so I kept my comments to myself. At least on day one of sampling.

"Josef, it's okay to be nervous," I said, projecting my own feelings and wanting to protect him. "It's my first time out here, too."

"I'm not *nerwwou*s," he said in his thick Czech accent. "I'm *cooh*l." He was lying through his tiny size Chiclet teeth.

Scrawny Josef reminded me of my brother Tom, who we nick-named "Bones." With a grin, Tom would flex his little biceps and suck in his belly to show a full rack of protruding ribs. When I was in third grade, I became more conscious that life was a little harder for him. I walked to the local public school, while Tom, sporting black, thick-rimmed glasses, rode a mini bus and attended a different school. Older boys called him "Four-eyes," "Retard," and "Sped" (special education), while the girls wrote him letters. The contents were usually along the lines of, "Tom, you are the cutest boy in the gym," with a big heart drawn around it. Strangers saw a healthy, handsome kid that loved fast cars, big trucks, and cute girls like most other boys, and didn't know he struggled with mild learning disabilities. He could throw a baseball like a star but couldn't fasten a zipper or tie his shoes until a year after most kids his age. Even as an adult, he didn't like lists or long instructions. I can still hear the frustration in his voice, "Jeez, one thing at a time!" or "Gosh, write it down!" Once as a preteen, Mom sent him to the store for three things, but when he rode his bike home he only had one item.

"Tom, I didn't want a gallon of milk," Mom said.

Knowing he had gotten it wrong, but trying hard to please, he replied, "Well, I couldn't remember, so I figured it was milk."

In the 1970s there were no clear diagnoses and fewer educa-tional programs for Tom. He was grouped into classes with kids with severe mental and physical disabilities and those with behav-ioral issues—all just one lump sum of a school's problem. After flying blind through his whole childhood, it wasn't until after high school when he went through psychological testing and evaluation, so our family could better understand him and try to help him. The doctors discovered his brain had a void in the right frontal lobe (responsible for judgment, problem-solving and emotion) and an injured temporal lobe (controls some learning and memory). The doctors owed it to the use of forceps during his difficult delivery; in the end, they took him by caesarean section. Now the doctors estimated that he'd "remain mentally and emotionally about thirteen." Pure-hearted and honest, he didn't know how to manipulate others or recognize when they took advantage of him, as had happened all too often. His brain damage also caused him to have a temper, organic and unprovoked, and partially explained why he'd been acting out more often.

Looking back, I often asked of the challenges he faced, Why him? Why not me? I wished I'd known to be a more patient and understanding sister. Life wasn't fair for him. I was first born. I got the best bedrooms when we moved, first dibs on the shower before the hot water ran out, shotgun in the car, and I swindled him out of his Halloween chocolates by trading my quantity for his quality. Maybe he would have liked sports, where he could bat away the aggression life had thrown at him. I could have encouraged him more, treated him better, taught him more as I figured out life myself. And though we'd fought almost daily during childhood, I was also his biggest defender.

"It's not his fault. He can't help it. Leave him alone!" I'd say, sometimes from afar, other times with a fist raised to strike his tormentor.

If anyone made fun of Tom, pushed him off his Evel Knievel bike, stole his skateboard or baseball mitt, said mean things, or made him cry for any reason at all, I was his Popeye against any Bluto bullies.

But I had left him to his own defenses back in Missouri. I wouldn't be there to coach him anymore. I moved away to seek peace, my own success and happiness, while he stumbled to find his way alone. I was like a twin in the womb who used up too much of the oxygen, leaving the weaker sibling with not nearly enough. I felt guilty for packing up my hobo bag and running away, leaving Tom behind.

Now on the ship, I'd defend Josef if needed. Together we walked tall through the processing area, gangster tough, masking our feelings of inadequacy. We knew we had to.

The Japanese factory foreman brushed past me like an ambulance, twirling his finger in the air, yelling, "High speedo! Hubba hubba!" I veered right in his gust. He insisted the crew bring in the gear, process, and pack faster. Always faster. A full crew could process up to 50,000 fish a day, and the boat could hold over 325 tons of frozen product. How many weeks would it take to fill our freezer? No one knew the answer—there were too many variables.

I pressed forward to the bow where I'd sample.

Many times in life, I've felt that I had to prove myself to men. I competed against guys on the basketball court. I baited my own hooks and released or filleted the fish I caught. While camping, I put up the tent, chopped the wood, and started the fire. Nocturnal creatures and howls didn't faze me. I changed my truck's oil, spark plugs, and flat tires, just like Walter taught me to. Though in my high school shop class I tried unsuccessfully to strike up an arc in welding and repeatedly got the electrode stuck to whatever metal I tried to weld, I could turn out wood projects on a lathe as well as the guys. I could hammer, saw, drill, dig, fix, and build. But this time, on this boat, I wasn't sure I could prove myself.

Two deckhands retrieved the fish from the starboard hatch, an opening taller and wider than a sliding glass door. The waves met us at eye level. I had to pay attention. Dean pierced each P-cod with the gaff and ripped them from the hooks. The miles of empty groundline wound amidship to the stern, where it was recoiled and repaired for the next set. Every man had a job to do. The fish traveled down blood-streaked conveyor belts, known less affectionately as the "slime line," for processing. The fish were first beheaded with saw blades, sliced open with knives, and then two crewmen, nicknamed "gut suckers," removed the innards with a metal scraper and suction hose. Further down the line, the fish were packed in metal pans according to size and species and transferred to a multilayered plate freezer. The blocks of fish came out like frozen sheet cakes and were then cased up—enclosed in cardboard boxes, wrapped in a paper bag, and stamped with the vessel's name—and stored below deck in the freezer hold until delivery. The factory had the strong, oily smell of fresh codfish, not pungent and putrid as I'd expected.

At my sampling station in the bow, I hung my scale on a rusty overhead pipe and laid the measuring board on the frigid steel counter. Whap, whap, whap. The dazed fish flopped from hooks to gaff to the conveyor belt. "Can't is not a word!" was replaced with "What if I do this wrong?" and "What if I look weak?"

I stood frozen, as if I were in front of a class trying to solve a complex organic chemistry problem. Doubt and nausea filled the voids between each trough and crest. I'd learned to keep my eyes on the horizon to avoid seasickness, but half of our time was spent in the wave's trough, my mind's eye in a constant state of vertigo, unable to see the thin line of a horizon. I might just puke all over the factory floor. Was it possible to barf away my anguish?

I stood at the open hatch. From inside the factory, I couldn't see the sheets of ice encasing every external surface of our ship, but I knew they were there, weighing us down. I removed my earplugs, tapped green-eyed Dean and a hooded Larone on the shoulder, shouting above the boisterous factory noise, "Hey guys. I'm all set! Could you fill my sample basket with what comes up next on the line?"

The tall, hooded one turned to face me, and I happily realized that there had been a substitute at the pole gaff. Russell, the anchor slinger, had taken Larone's spot. Dean jumped in and slowed the line. "Anything for you Darlin'," he said.

"Yeah, *anything*," added Russell, glancing at Dean.

Wait. It was noisy in the factory. Did I hear Dean right? Did he just call me "Darlin'?" I'm a tower of power. More gunpowder than powder puff. Not the spring-loaded, plastic, stick-legged ballerina inside a music box that easily folds under a closing lid. You never see a spinning, ponytailed tomboy wearing man-boots in those music boxes. But now Dean had called me Darlin,' a cutesy name. Maybe I'd grow to like it?

Dean heaped on the fish until my basket overflowed. The processors studied me as I attempted to solve a physics problem. I could pump some iron, but how would I manage a clean-and-press with a basket load of fish against the rolls of the boat? Was it possible to lift the full basket off the ground, juggle the two attached flaccid ropes, and target the hook swinging from the pendulum-like scale without stumbling or falling?

As I stood between two deckhands and the brimming basket of fish, I felt defeated before any physical exertion began. Maybe I couldn't do this? Clearly, I wasn't as strong as Russell the muscle, able to sling a fifty-pound anchor around like a small bag of groceries. Nor could my hands under the tension of the rope be as tough as Dean's. I became very aware of his strong hands earlier when he swiped his roughened palm against mine in a high five. His fingernails were dirty from hard work, his thumb muscle fat and meaty like a drumstick, his skin calloused. Man hands. Mine would never be like that.

The gusts of wintery wind at my back made me shiver. My cheeks and lips felt numb, as if I'd been shot with Novocain. Despite the thick gloves and my XtraTufs, I could barely feel my fingers and toes; they'd turned into popsicles. But I wouldn't let any of the twenty-five fishermen see me as uncertain or weak. I removed my gloves to warm my fingers, buy time, have a good whimper on the inside, and come up with a plan. I gathered my thoughts and wondered why I felt the need to be as strong as the guy next to me—until I looked down again at the plastic basket of fish at my feet. That's why. Cod, I see lots of Pacific cod, with bellies soft and round, layer upon layer, pressed out from my sample, suffocating from their own weight.

"Slow the line, Dean," said a gentle voice above the whine of the gear.

Russell, my knight in shining orange rain gear, came to my side.

"Try this," he suggested as he bent over and effortlessly lifted the basket of fish to the counter. Then he placed the ropes on the scale's hook and lowered the load. The dial swung around wildly. Why didn't I think of that? I caught myself looking straight into his eyes, admiring him and thinking, *He's so nice.* I forced my mind back to the task—to the fish. "I've seen other observers do it this way," he explained. "Also, don't let us overfill the baskets. Dean was jerking your chain by piling on the fish too high." He returned to his pole gaff duty, sped up the line, and said, "If you need *anything*, just ask."

Chocolate. I could use some chocolate.

A small bit of relief melted a chunk of ice from my frozen body. In this dangerous, alien world, at least one crewman was looking out for me, even if not for pure altruism. But for now, Russell put me at ease, and I could temporarily lower my protective shield a few inches.

For each haul I hoisted ten-plus baskets of fish to the scale and measured the length of each one to determine the species composition. I needed at least 350 kilograms (770-plus pounds) per sampled haul and had to weigh at least sixty of each dominant species and fifteen of each nondominant species. Some P-cod could be longer than my thirty-three-inch inseam, weigh up to fifty pounds, and reach eighteen years old. I hadn't lifted fish that big since unloading mahi-mahi off a sport fishing boat in the Outer Banks of North Carolina. A bad day for a codfish, we ripped them by their lips from the sea. I grabbed one by the open, fist-sized mouth and gills and swung it around like I had reeled it in with a pole myself. Once onboard, cod paled from gold to beige as compared to the marlin, sailfish, and dolphinfish we pulled from North Carolina's warm, turquoise Gulf Stream whose iridescent colors quickly faded to dull gray while the life and blood literally drained out of them.

As I sorted my sample, I came across a couple of orange rock-fish. I could barely look past their bulging eyes, ready to pop like bubble wrap, making me recall the sad eyes of that three-legged pug at the veterinary clinic. As deepwater fishes, like rockfish and cod, are quickly hauled to the surface, the gases in their blood, tissues, and swim bladders expand faster than can naturally be released. In addition to pop-out eyes, their bellies bloat, and their distended stomachs and intestines sometimes expel out of their mouths, gills, or vents (aka, anuses). Regardless of spewed guts, I had to determine the species. Likely they were shortraker or rougheye rockfish.

I thought back to the tough fish ID exam, my final test in observer training. Twenty fish and crabs were laid out on cold steel laboratory tables. Most of them had been dead and frozen for a while, not fresh like I'd see them onboard. I had to recall the genus and species from memory or use a dichotomous key. The key is an identification guide that separates physical traits into two classifi-cations, successively forking and becoming more specific as each characteristic is observed. The first fish was fleshy, flaccid, and narrow with small scales and an olive-gold mottled back. It had to be a pollock. Nothing else like it. Next, I studied the nearly straight lateral line and right-eyed orientation of the thin, bony-headed flat-fish. Did the mouth extend to *below* or *past* the eye? Flathead sole, I think. The last specimen was another flatfish: arrowtooth flounder or Greenland turbot? Which species had the ninety-degree angled preoperculum (the anterior bony flap that covers their gills) and not the rounded one? The turbot. I knew it.

Now in the fish factory, my heart rate increased as I approached an orange, bass-like rockfish. There were many species of rockfish, only subtly different from one another, so difficult to identify. My gloveless fingers fluttered through the pages of the key. I counted the pin-prick dorsal rays. Two processors said in agreement, "They're rougheye rockfish." I felt for raspy spines below the front of their swollen eyes. Confirmed. Rougheye rockfish. The guys were right. To my surprise, they were helping me.

I sorted the fish by species and measured each of their fork lengths (the length from the tip of their snout to the middle rays of their caudal fin or tail). They slid across the chilled steel counter. I struggled to wrangle the grease pencil in one clumsy gloved hand and a clipboard in the other; all of it, including myself, covered in fish slime. I recorded the sample weight on my plastic data sheet: twenty-two kilograms, just under fifty pounds. The fish kept coming aboard, one after the other in a steady rhythm. My back weakened under heavy lifting. Twenty. Fifty. Eighty pounds. Each additional basketful felt like one hundred pounds. Fat fish after fish. I gripped, measured, and tossed. My hands grew stiff.

The processors watched me, and I wondered if I was doing it correctly. Were my totals accurate? Would I break down or break in half? Later, I would extrapolate the average lengths and weights of my random sub-sample to calculate overall catch tonnage and report my findings as part of my weekly catch report. We would keep the pace around the clock, haul by haul, and week by week. I was only beginning to see why commercial fishing ranked as one of the world's most hazardous occupations.

I had stumbled through my first haul sample and hoped for future hauls I'd be able to properly identify the fish and do my job well. Before exiting the factory, one of the crew pulled himself from the processing line. "Button up," he said, then grabbed the high pressure, icy-saltwater-fed fire hose and blasted the slime off my rain gear. I just smiled.

In the first week I felt an innate connection to this foreign place, much like when I scubadived on a coral reef for the first time during college. My eyes had been opened to a whole new planet, separate from land, and far different from anything I'd experienced, right down to the air I breathed. This nomadic lifestyle, the bare-bones living conditions, tons of fish, the constant movement of the ocean, and, most of all, my twenty-five male shipmates completely over-whelmed me. I predicted my whole contract would be full of tests and flirtations and a guessing game of who I could trust. Would I need to protect weaker crewmen like I'd done for my younger brother, or would I be the one in need of protection? I wanted to let down my guard, but was afraid *friendly* would be misinterpreted as *flirty*. Mostly, I looked forward to the hard work ahead of me. Fishing and life on the high seas had, at least for the moment, cap-tured me.

8

~~~

CAMARADERIE

BOYS. Guys. Men. Dudes. My brother. Most of my life, I've planted myself among the male gender: in shop class or garages loaded with tools, under car hoods and much too heavy free weights at the gym. However, being near them wasn't enough; I needed to be in the middle of them—the dogpile, the sport court, a wrestling match, a flag football game. I valued their strength, a characteristic our culture prized in men, but not in women. Now I lived among some of the roughest. It would take me weeks to feel comfortable with sampling and much longer to snug in tightly into this sardine can of men.

In Seattle, before my contract began, I expected to be aboard ship with plenty of time for camaraderie. What else was there to do all day and night on an ice-encased island of steel except do my job and get to know my twenty-five closest shipmates? I imagined the guys and I would spend hours hip-to-hip in the galley passing condiments around the table and watching crime dramas and action movies over shared plates of nachos and bags of microwave popcorn. In the galley over a meal or in the factory over conveyor belts of headless fish, we'd be in full exchange of the intimate details of our lives . . . or so I'd thought.

In stark contrast to my storybook imagination, social hour and recreation were excluded from this Alaskan cruise package. The guys were divided between sixteen-hour, two-packs-of-cigarettes, around-the-clock shifts. In their eight hours off, they only had time to eat, shower, and sleep. They occasionally gave up precious snooze time for frivolous entertainment, like movies, card games, books, or talking with me. I'm sure such sacrifice didn't apply often toward male observers.

In the first few weeks we all suffered from a rigorous schedule, lack of sleep, and ice cold temperatures. Continuous standing, gripping, tossing, and gear mending caused frequent and severe muscle cramps. We all took a beating, eternally braced in some off-kilter knee bend, squat, or pseudo-yoga pose and ready to make futile grasps at a flat wall or anything solid. At sea, pain is an inconvenience. There is no rest at will. No days off. No calling in sick. No whining. You work or you are fed to the sharks: your peers.

Green-eyed Dean often tried to elicit my compassion. "Laura, my hands and legs are *killing* me. How about massaging them for me? Real quick. Come on, Darlin'. Please?" I was good at giving massages, having been raised by a mother with chronic pain, who frequently said, "Massage my back." Dean softly swiped his rough palm and work-stained fingers, eager to be held, into mine. Like a sad-eyed puppy at the pound, he pleaded with an open invitation. "Laura, it'll only take a minute." It would take less time for me to make a bad decision.

I mentally battled with the image of my hands around his tight, bulging muscles. I would love to give any of his body parts a massage, but training had sealed the temptation and filed it away as off-limits. The instructor reminded us, "Fraternizing with the crew is a no-no." With a nonchalant eye roll, I pulled away from

Dean, "Go talk to Hobey. He'll lube you up with his blue bottle of cure-all."

Hobey, the granola boy mate, had a natural remedy for everything. He chased us with his warming oil scented with a combination of juniper, rosemary, lavender, and sage. Every week he asked, "Laura, do you have your period yet? Ginger tea relieves cramps." As much as I wanted some level of closeness with the crew, Hobey was a bit too personal right out of the gate.

"Pop some potassium," I said to Dean, knowing the mineral reduces muscle cramping. "Or eat some bananas." Sadly, out of superstition, having bananas—along with plastic honey bears, and women—aboard was considered bad luck. I stowed my urge to help, knowing one innocent shoulder rub, a single touch, or even the friendly side-hug I so desperately wanted to give and receive would tip the scale too far. I could only offer my empathy and a few ibuprofens.

Dean turned away with a smirk, rejected for the moment but still undefeated. I let out a sigh of relief, both worried and thrilled by the notion of my eroding fortitude. He knows, I thought. He knows I can be worn down.

In college I had surrounded myself with a tight circle of idealistic, pure-hearted boys who held me upright and cushioned me between them like buoys, never allowing me to fall very far or very hard. They had warned me that most men interpret friendship with women as something more than friendship. Grandma's words of warning from my youth echoed in my head, "Don't let those boys *put the make* on you!" and "A man should re*spect* you." Polish Pa would raise a fist to the men aboard and shout, "Summ-omm-bitch, I k*iii*ll you! Stay away from my granddaughter!"

Mom, on the other hand, was either my quarterback or a blocker. She would find the hunkiest lifeguard at the beach and say, "My daughter over there likes your tan. Can you go tell her what type of tanning oil you use?" (Thanks, Mom, for the awkward introduction, but works for me, because now I'm talking to a lifeguard with a perfectly carved chest and quads.) But if a real date showed up at our front door, she'd greet him with piercing eyes and a half-smile and ask, "What are your intentions young man?" She'd invade his personal space, getting as close as possible, and whisper, "Just remember, you hurt my daughter, you hurt me. You don't want to hurt me. Have her back before midnight. Nothing good goes on after midnight." A fact she knew all too well from her years as a bartender.

My small family, my wild pack of hyenas, had shielded me from becoming a boy toy, but they weren't here now. I had moved to Seattle to get away from the hovering cloud of chaos, and until now I hadn't realized they'd also been my protectors. I had no buffer at sea, and desperately hoped I wouldn't need one.

Fortunately, my schedule was more flexible than the crew's. I could take a break when I needed one. I sampled the beginning of one haul and the end of the next, which allowed me to sleep for six or so hours in between. And though the shipboard routines were hard for all of us to master, they were broken up by bits of unusual fun scattered between the factory and the wheelhouse.

Small rituals and friendship dawned between me and some of the crew. Jazz served as my alarm clock. First, I'd hear the loathsome whine of the gear, signaling a haulback. Then, in the dark, beyond my blue curtain, Jazz pawed and smacked at my feet, buried deep in my sleeping bag. "Hey. Haulback," he said like a military drill sergeant. "Get up!" Sometimes he said, "Hey, it's *Aaa*nchor Time!" I guess I'd made it obvious that watching the guys (okay, specifically Russell) bring in the anchor *really* turned my crank. Jazz's foot shakedown, like a sibling pulling the blankets off the bed on a cold winter's day, was probably all the physical contact I'd get on this boat without it being perceived as crossing the line. The thought of leaving my cocoon-like sleeping bag to layer up so

I could stand behind Captain Gabe for hours with my face out the window or step into a factory exposed to blasts of frigid air was entirely unmotivating. Would I ever get used to the constant vibration of the vessel, the cold, the around-the-clock sampling, and the strange sleep patterns?

At zero-dark-thirty every morning I grappled for my sweats and pulled them on lying prostrate in my rack. My third roommate, who I had nicknamed Cool Boy, slept in the top bunk across from me. When we awoke at the same time, he sat up in his bunk and whispered my name, the volume escalating each time, "Laura, LaURA, LAURA. Let me guess. The sky is dark. The seas are rough. It's cold. It's wet."

I high-fived him and recited back my own mantra, reminding myself why I was here: "Seize the day! Seize the gray! Seize the pay!" Cha-ching.

Cool Boy, young and frisky, usually had something flirty but innocent to say. Before I exited the room he smiled and said, "Laura, I know what you need. You need a good black man like me." I laughed, thinking he was right, but he wasn't the black man I had my eyes on. But crew relations were strictly prohibited. An at-sea fling wasn't worth the trouble, even though trouble seemed inevitable with this rowdy crowd. I wanted a relationship someday, but I was at sea to make money and sort out my future, not give in to frivolous temptations.

Stumbling into the wheelhouse each new day, I met Captain Gabe's lit up eyes and greeting, "Well, good morning Little Miss Snacky Cakes!" I don't know where the name came from, but I found humor in it, not disrespect, and it stuck.

My reply, "Good morning, Captain Crabby Pants," or "Ahoy, Captain Crummy Weather," reflected the mood of the day. The regularity of our ridiculous greetings brought me joy as the number of sunrises and quantity of fish tallied up.

The morning routine would continue with me cranking down the stiff window with two hands and hawking a big loogie into the waves.

To which he'd wrinkle his face and blurt out, "That's disgusting!" while hiding a smile.

"You know you love it, and that's why I do it." This tradition marked the beginning of each day, like the punch of a time clock. It also provided true intimacy and bonding with a guy on a fishing boat.

I suspected I was Gabe's first female loogie-hawker. He was a put-together, educated, golden boy from San Francisco. An elite breed, he earned his Unlimited Third Mates License through a maritime academy, and increased his credentials to an Unlimited Chief Mate's and a 5,000 Ton Fishing Industry Master's License, about three times bigger than needed to run this vessel. He worked aboard cargo ships, tankers, and research ships, then later decided on a career in commercial fishing, where he could make *big* money. At the time, a captain could potentially earn more than twenty-five grand a month, but only high risk, responsibility, and stress were guaranteed.

Captain Gabe spoke sternly to his crew and earned their respect, but he lacked the tough guy routine I'd expected from a Bering Sea captain. He was sensitive; not a girlie-man, but an I-can-talk-about-a-woman's-period sensitive. But he was equally comfortable churning out cuss words, belying his refined demeanor and intellect. I think he swore to fit in with the crew, but his curses came out sounding surfer-Shakespearean, "Thou ought not to be an asshole, Dude."

It was there, nestled inches behind him at the helm, perched two levels above the factory with a bird's-eye view of the line, in tight quarters for hours upon hours a day that I absorbed his command and sea sense. It is where we befriended, and sometimes annoyed, each other.

I suspected that not all captains welcomed their observers to hang out in the wheelhouse. After I sampled, clowned with the guys on the line, or helped Jazz cook, the bridge is where I wanted to be. It was the exclusive lounge on the top floor with the penthouse view. You wanted to go, because it was *up there*. It housed the head honcho, *El Jefe*, *El Capitan*. His power and authority elevated above the minions from the bridge. The doorway closed to all except the privileged—the mate, engineers, and, in this case, me.

From the beginning, I'd been trying to figure out my place among the wolf pack. I sensed the crew hierarchy, a sort of entrenched caste system based on job position and pay. The total trip profit, minus expenses like fuel and food, was paid out in percentages according to one's crew share. The men were paid according to rank, merit, and experience. I had always believed that one's value is in their person, not in their performance or job title. Here, however, the higher the position, the greater the risk and responsibility, the more value and esteem they seemed to hold, and pay was the reward.

At the bottom of the pay scale were the factory processors, where most fishermen started. They were further separated by duty: the slime line (beheaders and gut suckers); the sorters (by grade, color and size); the packers (weighing, packaging, and labeling the product); and the "case up" freezer crew. All had to clean the equipment. Newer crew received only a fraction of a share: one-quarter or maybe a half.

The deckhands ascended up the food chain, and with increased risk came one-plus crew shares. After a few years of experience they could work their way up to earn a shot at the envied position of deck boss, like a deckhand team captain. The deckhands flowed in steady sync with the gear, from the stern to repair and reset the line, and into the bow to retrieve it. Only a special few could haul up the anchor and draw the coveted gaze of the female observer.

Jazz, in his white chef's shirt, stood in a class by himself, with allegiance weighted toward the crew but housed in the neutral territory of the galley.

Two engineers, the tall, sinewy chief with a cowlick on the starboard side of his beard and his squat, near silent assistant worked sixteen-hour shifts, overlapping one another for four hours. They spent most of their time in the engine room muffled under ear protection or occupied by the latest blinking light, shrieking alarm, or equipment failure.

Captain Gabe, Hobey the mate, and Yuki-san, the Japanese fish master, worked sixteen-hour days like everyone else, but manned the helm for at least eight hours and spent the rest of their time in the factory or servicing the latest problem. Fish masters historically knew the Bering Sea well since the early JV (joint venture) days when foreign vessels co-fished with Americans, before the fisheries became more regulated and domestic. They also tend to be experts in the various cuts of fish sold to Japan and Asian markets and usually ruled over the factory. Many vessels hired them to keep the knowledge that had been passed on to them.

Hobey, who shared a stateroom with Gabe and worked the night shift, tended to be more "in" with the crew than the captain. The mate was never quite in control, didn't like to be told what to do, and thought he knew better than anyone else. I wouldn't take sides. I wanted to be ranked not above or below anyone, but beside them, to roam freely between the wheelhouse to galley to factory to be viewed as their equal. I realized my gender trumped all rank, and found nearly all welcomed my attention.

The captain might have earned the most pay, but it was lonely at the top. He was the chief risk-taker, decision-maker, and manager of the magic that happens between the wheelhouse and a freezer full of fish. Ultimately, he held all our lives in his heavily burdened hands. He also took the brunt of blame when times got tough—problems with the gear, poor weather, few fish, too much bycatch, a less-than-expected paycheck, long trips, and why you were unable to get home in time to witness the birth of your first child. It didn't matter. It was his fault. Always.

Gabe usually spent his time steering the course, hauling or setting gear, or charting our next position. He often bantered over the radio with other captains. Other times, in silence, he decoded covert conversations between rival ships. His direct orders came in via fax or ship-to-shore radio from someone sitting in a warm Seattle office with a notebook. Between tasks, he did what the sea called all of us to do in a quiet moment—daydream into the horizon or stargaze into the darkness and bounce our deepest hopes and thoughts off the universe and God. Noticing his lost look at times, I wondered what thoughts captivated him.

I saw how he set the tone and spirit of the ship. Nearly tied to the wheelhouse most of the time, it was hard for him to make small talk and socialize with the crew on a regular basis. But a couple of times a day he'd leave Hobey or Yuki-san at the helm and pass through the factory. On a poor catch day, he'd stroll through with his hands in his pockets and smile encouragingly. On a high yield day, he'd throw up fist pumps to motivate, support, and praise. Other times, he'd rush through the line disappointed and bark orders like a drill sergeant.

One night, he and I were engaged in one of our rituals: jamming to the likes of Chaka Khan and Mary J. Blige while scanning the horizon for the elusive *green flash*. I wasn't sure if it was a real phenomenon, as I had yet to witness the spot above the sun quickly change color at sunset. Maybe it was the point between water and sky at which we all vanished? Still, I was in search of skyscapes and reflections by the moon, stars, and sun to spark our dark days.

Just as Hobey showed up to the bridge for the changing of the guards, Captain Gabe interrupted our hearty fun and laughter. He tapped his watch, and said, "Well, it's about that time. I have to go down to the factory and yell at a few people." This is what many captains interpret as control. When a crewman would ask me, "What'd you do to the Skipper? What's he got up his ass tonight?" Gabe had succeeded. He couldn't be too nice and shine his wide dimpled grin too often or he'd be labeled a pantie-waist. I guessed the crew had a derogatory nickname for him, though I was unaware of any at this point.

Later that evening, Hobey hauled back another set. Lights shined down on the incoming line while I tallied a third of the catch, as required. I often had to psyche myself up to finish sampling in the factory. The industrial lights seemed more invasive at night, blinding me like high beams in a dark tunnel. Though my job and the pace of the factory was the same at all hours, I preferred to sample in the day, when I might catch a glimpse of a whale, the changing weather, a rainbow, or another ship in the distance. And though the daylight hours would increase the closer we drew to summer, the numbers on the clock and my sample scale blurred together with each passing day at sea.

Before I finished phase two of sampling in the factory that night, I sat slouched in the brown vinyl chair in the center of the wheelhouse with my hands curled around the simple luxury of a mug of hot chocolate. At times I'd enter the bridge to see the chief engineer sitting in the chair and felt like a dad arriving to see his La-Z-Boy already occupied in front of the TV. Roles, norms, and boundaries were becoming established, and they were happy to surrender it to me.

Outside it was midnight pitch black, except the light of the moon poking through the cloud layer and the gantry lights shining behind us. Inside, the array of instruments—the radar, a plotter, electronic charts, GPS, small screens on the SSB (single side band) and VHF radios, a depth sounder, a factory camera—lit the wheelhouse like the dim flicker of candles in a power outage. Scarce radio chatter, broken by a few crackles reminded me of the miles between me and land. Night after night in the ever-changing Bering Sea, I sat there embraced by my chair in a dark wheelhouse, looking out while scanning my past and searching inward. For peace. For answers. For strength.

As I peeled back my layers, I realized the island I was becoming couldn't always stand alone. I yearned for a relationship, true love . . . if there was such a thing. In my recent past, I listened to an inner voice, a strong voice, that said, "Keep walking. Keep looking. Next!" I believed a trustworthy someone would come along and we'd click together like missing puzzle pieces. I wouldn't need to be the foundation to hold us up before we crumbled. He'd be resilient enough for both of us. I wasn't sure if it was Luke in Florida. I didn't think it could realistically be Russell, even though he had my attention and Captain Gabe said he was "sweet on me." I looked into the water for a floating Magic 8-Ball to predict my future and guide me on the next steps to take on land. Nothing but foam and white caps. *Reply Hazy. Ask Again Later.*

I continued to spend hours and hours, days and nights, in the factory to sample each haul, slowly getting to know some of the crew, my real quarry. Talk. Banter. Jests and gesticulations. A minute to listen here. Another minute to chat there. Each person a cog in a fast-paced, orderly machine with a job to do. But I couldn't disrupt their focus, the steady flow of fish moving from hooked lines, through saw blades, over conveyors, and into metal sheet pans and freezers. I had my role, too, a mere legality really to the captain and crew. The fishing operation didn't technically *need* me to function. The crew probably viewed me as the annoying bird in the Cuckoo clock, tapping them on the shoulder and popping out with my gear every so often to say, "Fill my basket. Fill my basket." Sampling by their sides mostly ran smoothly, until I showed up and

The longliner safely docked in Seattle.

The Coast Guard would use this Jacob's ladder to board at sea if they chose us for an inspection.

The COMSAT equipment on the left was used to send my weekly catch reports to the Seattle office.

Newly coiled skates ready
for squid bait.

Anchor time!

The food storage room . . .
and scene of "the bite."

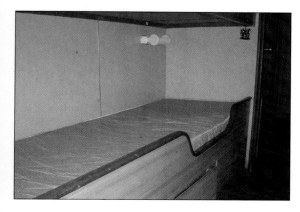

The cook's bunk below mine.

Sampling the catch.

This is a tunnel to one of the World War II bunkers lining the hillsides of Dutch.

I'd like to eat this crab.

An assortment
of Alaskan catch.

Holy Ascension
Orthodox Church
cemetery on the north
side of Unalaska Island.

Happy to be portside in Dutch Harbor.

An international tramper in the bay ready to receive fish for transport.

Seattle bound. Mount Ballyhoo in the background.

Gumby survival suit practice in my studio apartment the night before my departure to the Bering Sea.

Clowning around with a life ring.

World War II bunker on Dutch hillside.

The view from inside a World War II bunker on Dutch hillside.

The most civilized place in Dutch, the airport.

I would blend in with the guys in this outfit.

An international tramper in the bay ready to receive fish for transport.

Attempting to save some birds who were swept onto the vessel after a "bird storm."

An octopus, one of the many specimens I brought to the galley to challenge the cook. This one crawled off deck and freed itself.

Sometimes one has the urge to put an octopus on their head while at sea.

The crew is busy repairing coils for the next set in the stern, where much mischief occurs.

The hatch where they bring in the fish on the line. Do they part the line or hack off the tail of a giant sleeper shark?

A decent weather day and a rare one with land in sight.

Buoy markers and a life raft on the upper deck.

Feeling extra tough in my XtraTufs, but ready for some flirty sandals.

Showing love for
measuring and weighing
Pacific cod.

Covered in fish slime.

Flashing an invertebrate
in my fave blue sweatshirt,
lost during an onboard bet.

A Bering Sea assortment.

My only privacy was
in my rack.

Me and my fellow
observer and new best
friend, Stephanie.

A big-headed cod calls for a ventriloquist act or a puppet show.

A midwater trawler iced up at the dock in Dutch.

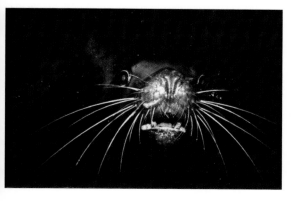

A Steller sea lion wants a snack, but it's illegal to feed them.

A variety of Bering Sea fish.

A wolf eel with vise-grip jaws.

Looking for some me time on deck.

Looking out a porthole in Dutch.

SS Northwestern, attacked by the Japanese in 1942, aground in Captain's Bay, Dutch Harbor.

Tramper in the bay ready to receive fish for transport.

Time to turn
and burn in
Dutch Harbor.

Mother-lode
haul of giant
shortraker
rockfish.

became the audience at a variety show, a freak show, or a peep show. Each day unveiling a new act.

While I measured and weighed out my sample, the guys earned my attention. One gutsucker on the processing line, Wade, a burly, long-haired biker-type, was king storyteller and poet. This talent transferred into ventriloquist acts through fish, especially with big-mouthed cod and ashy, devilish grenadiers or rattails with their obtuse heads, pointy noses, wide-set eyes, and long, tapered bodies. For Wade and others, they seemed more comfortable making up stories and talking through a fish puppet than to have a real heart-to-heart. By this time, I was okay talking to a fish or a puppet. My options were few.

Ed, another gutsucker, a big, pallid, plodding guy with a Frank-enstein blockhead might've been boxed between the ears a few too many times. A loose cannon and as unstable as I'd seen, Ed put me on edge. One minute he was in high spirits, high-strung, or maybe just high, and the next he towered over a crewman ready to fight. Daily, he'd say, "This sucks. I'm gonna quit this shit job." How-ever, Ed was particularly fond of Jazz, who he called his "brother from another mother." Jazz gave Ed a lot of the praise he seemed to need. When Ed wasn't raging or threatening to quit, he turned into a Saint Bernard, ready to pounce into your lap. He wanted to be everyone's buddy, for all to like him. He often rocked his hand on a guy's shoulder and said to the others, "He's good people," and laughed, "Huh, huh, huh." As my mom would say, "That guy is not playing with a full deck." He needed to lay off the narcotics and get a real prescription for something to help him focus.

One day, while I filled another blue basket with my eighty-five-pound sample, Ed juggled a couple of cod and a stray, snakelike eelpout like a jester. Then Ed slipped into an air-guitar show with a diamond-shaped arrowtooth flounder. He tossed it on the conveyor belt and said, "Man, I gotta take a m*eee*an whiz!" something my brother would've said. He turned around right in front of me in the factory and peed. Just like the lyrics of Ted Nugent's classic rock song, "When in doubt, I whip it out. Got me a rock and roll band; it's a free-for-all." The factory, and my new life in its confines, *was* a free-for-all. This was not the show I paid to see. Surely *this*, too, was not common practice. But I'm afraid it was. Annoyed, I said, "Um, excuse me!"

He turned his head. "What's the big deal? You gotta brother, don't ya? Ya gotta go when ya gotta go. Huh, huh, huh." I guessed I should be thankful, because he spared me from having to see his eelpout. A faint yellow stream washed below our feet on raised grates and out the scuppers with a slosh of fish offal and seawater. I hoped to avoid ever seeing floating loggers in the factory pool.

As I grabbed my sample basket, I took a breath and stepped back for a minute to see if I was being too sensitive. These were male fishermen after all. I was on their turf. That's what guys did. They peed standing. They also had to contend with all those layers of clothes and gear. Young and naïve, I was still learning how to handle the discomforts of life in general, but this environment was different. I wanted respect, but had to quickly decide when to react and when to brush things off. I was always guessing at what level to respond to their foible and folly. As Ed had said, "No big deal." I decided to look the other way. After all, what was I going to do about it? To what end would I snitch? Life here would not get easier with enemies.

I scanned my final overflowing sample. The prohibs—this time copper-colored deepwater tanner crabs with skinny legs—were still heaped atop the fish pile as I'd left them when Ed distracted me. But wait!

"Okay. Who took it?" I asked. "Who nabbed the red sea cucumber?" While I'd turned to watch Ed's performance, someone took the plump, football-sized invertebrate from my basket. I skimmed the factory processors for guilt and met a lineup of poker faces.

Wade the poet and storyteller chuckled behind a talking cod with flared gills, and snitched, "Akira ate it." Of course.

Akira, the Japanese factory foreman, and his cohorts, their faces peppered with stubble, smirked at me through the packing area window. Like a stern mother guarding a fresh batch of cookies, I barked, "You can only eat them *after* I sample them." I wrote down "one missing sea cucumber" on my data sheet. I shook my head sideways at them, "No. No. No." Still, I laughed at the absurdity of my daily challenges.

Like the days spent with this bunch of jokers, my samples were also filled with surprises. The incoming line often snagged oddities from the seafloor: an old-fashioned, hand-blown glass bottle; a rubber glove; a piece of black coral stemmed out and smooth as a barkless willow branch; brightly colored sea anemones tightened like sphincters trying to stay alive; a long piece of silky kelp; or a wiggling orange octopus. Sometimes I'd mildly reprimand the guys over the loudspeaker from the wheelhouse, "No batting practice with the starfish." They'd whack them with their gaffs to see who could hit the most seagulls, or "sea pukes," as they called them. Or they'd whip the pole gaff at the birds like living piñatas. Tagged salmon, though infrequent, were the most desired catch. The fish had been tagged to track their growth and how far they traveled. When one came in, you'd think the crew had won the lottery or found gold. They fought over who would get to send the tag back to NMFS or ADF&G to receive a reward: a T-shirt, baseball hat, or a five-dollar bill. The worst catch was another vessel's live gear, or ghost gear (crab pots, hooked line and nets), lost or left behind but continued to fish. The guys often tried to fool me with imaginary items, too. "Hey Laura, we pulled up a glove with fingers (or a boot with toes) today. Want it for your sample?" At times I fell for it, and my heart skipped a beat. Because so many ships go down in the rough Alaskan waters each year, the potential for pulling up a body part was real.

One day a buzz sped through the boat. The Japanese fish master, Yuki-san, ran down from the wheelhouse and into the factory twirling a green towel in the air and shouting, "Hubba hubba!" We'd hit the jackpot. A mother lode of giant shortraker rockfish. They were at least twice to quadruple the size of the fish we'd been catching. He twisted up the towel as customary and wrapped the Hachimaki (headband) around his permed hair to express perseverance, courage, and victory. He knelt on the floor to closely examine the bounty.

Sitting cross-legged in my rain gear, I watched in awe, then he placed the largest rockfish across my legs. It covered me. That one fish, over three feet long and fifty-plus pounds, was too big to force into my sample basket. The foreman saw dollar bills, at least one hundred of them, in my lap; I saw majestic, marine wildlife cradled dead in my lap. The fish could have easily been more than one hundred years old. After the adrenaline passed, I felt compassion for these granddaddy rockfish, just as I had for the animals healed and those lost at the vet clinic. It felt like we had killed the last elephant in the jungle. Their taking not only seemed wrong; we were absolutely wrong. After we hauled, processed, and began to pack much of the catch, we were told we'd made a mistake. We had accidentally drifted into a closed fishing area. All of the remaining fish on the line had to be retrieved and tossed overboard, because fish caught in a closed area is considered illegal and unretainable. We watched the ginormous fish bodies with bulging eyes float away with the crewmen's fat paychecks. I felt awful for them, but also for the fish.

Part of my job included the special cod stomach dissection project. The data was used to determine predation mortality and to better understand the food web. Cod stomachs, like human stomachs, are lined with undulating folds of rugae that stretch out to increase the surface area of a full stomach to aid digestion. I had to collect no more than five stomachs per haul across four size categories, and up to eighty by the end of my contract. I removed the constricted sacs, which look like tightly wrapped spring rolls full of fish and invertebrates, minus the mint and shredded carrots, and bagged them up. The cloth bags were immersed in 10 percent formalin, your basic embalming fluid, which left a dry, burning sensation in the back of my throat upon incidental inhale while also probably altering my DNA. In the bag I included a data tag with the fish's weight, fork length, sex, and whether or not it had spawned. Some stomachs had regurgitated out their mouths and were deemed unusable for sampling. Others, I accidently sliced open to reveal the half-digested, gnarled prey. Larger cod were piscivorous, eating mainly fish. Smaller cod were packed with invertebrates, amphipods, crab parts, and small pollock.

As I dissected the stomachs, the Japanese guys asked me, "Rora, what doing?" I gave them the "I'm watching you" look and waved my gloved finger at them. I intercepted their false passes at my abundant sample with a karate chop. These asides with the Japanese, along with teasing them about their inability to grow real man beards, became our playful ritual. Still, I had to shield my basket from their desire to salt, hang, dry, and eat my fresh-from-the-sea specimens.

Who knew this crew, my companions, would wreak such mischief on the average day? We were an oddball mix, like the random assortment of invertebrates in my sample basket. Each fisherman had a life story I might never know. I rooted for the guys to succeed, to catch a lot of fish and earn good pay for their hard labor. We were stuck with one another, doing our best under the circumstances. We could only escape to our bunks, our coffins of comfort, to rest it out until the next round of surprise incidents, the next weather pattern, and the next haulback. Sea was preparing me for something bigger in life, and some days were more trying than others.

9

NEVER GIVE UP

I sensed the incoming weather in the factory; I felt it in my stagger. Standing, walking, eating, sleeping—everything was harder in foul weather. Hordes of seagulls darted starboard as we turned into the shifting winds, but we had to finish. My stomach churned.

Suddenly we heard Captain Gabe over the loud-hailer, "Wave!" The guys jumped back from the open hatch. I steadied myself the best I could. A twenty-footer sideswiped us and funneled onto the factory floor. We pitched portside. Any of us could easily fall out of the hatch and be sucked down into the ocean. My sample basket surfed several feet across the floor. I thought, I made it this far on my own. I can do this. I'm not going to fall. No one will see me fall. I kept my knees loose, to help steady myself with the up and down of the waves. Frozen palms grasped tightly onto cold metal equipment, bracing ourselves from becoming human pinballs. The guys cussed aloud; secretly I prayed, and I hoped I wasn't alone. After the surge, we scanned the factory. Who bit it, and who was still standing? Was anyone injured? The crew immediately went back to business as usual. I realized this is just another normal day at sea to them. As for me I was adjusting, one wave at a time, trying to find my own bravery in the face of doubt and fear. I still couldn't believe I had chosen this.

I feared the wind most, silent until it came in contact with an object. It appeared from across the sea, gaining momentum along the way. The longer, farther, and faster the wind blew over open ocean, the bigger the waves became. Captain Gabe had explained, "There are normally two components to wave height: swells and seas. Swells are less of a factor in the Bering Sea because they are interrupted by land, but the seas caused by severe local wind can kick our asses just as hard. The waves tend to be shorter, steeper, and more violent here as compared to similar-sized waves in the North Pacific." The waves, as tall as two-story buildings, found us. Captain Gabe said they could grow even larger. Throughout the night they lifted and circled and tossed us, a tiny bobber, only to drop us back deep into the trough. With each wave we leaned over a little more. Where was the breaking point, when the ship couldn't right itself?

Whirl. Whoosh. We rode out the twisting jerk of a bronco. Pounding against frozen metal. Slam! Behold the power of a freight train. We were a house getting pushed off its foundation. A life shaken . . . rattled . . . unhinged.

In my bunk, I stuffed clothes beneath the edges of my mattress to reduce the sway and to buffer me from jostling against the hard, raised borders of my rack. I chocked myself in with one bruised knee against the wall and my other foot pressed tight to the opposite side. I held onto the feeling you get seconds before a car accident, when you hammer—hard—on the brakes. Every muscle cringed, stiffened, and braced for impact. I squinched my eyes and clenched my teeth, trying to keep my head from snapping loose from my neck. I clasped my hands together and prayed hard, so hard God would hear me above the sound of the angry waves and the eerie howl.

I couldn't work. I couldn't sleep. But there in my dark bunk, was where I should find comfort and rest like a baby in a crib, sheltered from rough weather. Instead, the cradle rocked with each wave. Incessantly. My thoughts swung like a pendulum from the gripping fear of death to those of gratitude and hope. Many nights I pleaded, "Dear God, please. Please calm the seas. Please let me sleep. I'm so tired." Another plea with every side-to-side roll of a wave and shift of the wind. Sometimes a colossal wave would swipe us, sending a tremor through the whole boat . . . and then it was gone. "Thank you, God, for saving us."

I've begged and praised in similar prayers throughout my life. This night, filled with fear of the storm, I forced my thoughts elsewhere. To land. To hope. Through the most fearful moments of my life, I've also felt the most grateful.

I thought back to my first month in Seattle. Surrounded by strangers in a town I didn't know, I felt I'd made the wrong decision. But encouragement, like doubt, comes in many disguises. While putting new Washington license plates on my truck, I heard "Zooooom!" A gaunt man, his hair awry, rolling toward me on a fully loaded shopping cart. A cardboard sign stating, "Will work for money or food," blew up into his face. He laughed and halted at my back tires.

"Hey, let me help you. Don't sit on the street. Here's my coat," he offered, placing the torn bomber jacket on the ground by my side.

In the next thirty minutes, I discovered Lucas had been taken from his mom at age eight and was tossed between multiple boys' homes and foster homes.

"'Crick Neck" is what they call me on the street," he said by way of introduction. His muscles permanently shortened, stiff, and tight along the right side of his thin collar. "I have something wrong with my brain." So did my little brother, I thought. He admitted, "I can't read or write."

Lucas was twenty-eight, only a few years older than me, but street life had aged him by ten years. He lived day-to-day, panhandling and doing odd jobs. He avoided loitering and receiving handouts from The Mission and other homeless shelters. Like me, he wanted to survive on his own.

"I don't go to the shelters. Too many troublemakers there that do crimes and beat me up," he explained, tightening the screw through my license plate.

They wouldn't have beat him up if I'd been there. I would have defended him like my own brother. Lucas' frame was thin. He ate, on average, only a burrito or corndog every other day.

Everyone wants to love and be loved, and Lucas was no exception. He said he dated, but the girls broke up with him, because he didn't "put out." He and I had that in common.

Lucas shared some advice: "Respect the elderly. Open your heart. Be honest. Believe in God." I etched his wise words in my journal that night.

My problems were small compared to the struggles Lucas faced.

"Do you ever lose hope because of the tough times you go through?" I asked him.

"I only look at the good," he said, stretching his neck to look up at me with his eyes.

The angel of perspective showed up just when I needed him.

I stood up. "I have to go Lucas." I felt guilty to have an apartment when Lucas lived on the street. I felt guilty for leaving my family in Missouri, especially my brother who was working hard to make it on his own. "I don't have any food or money on me to give you, Lucas."

"The best thing you could've done was to talk to me," he replied.

I felt the same.

I pulled a Mexican wool blanket and an Army-green canteen from my truck and placed them in his arms. He latched the canteen to his belt, kissed my hand, and hugged me goodbye. I wondered where he was off to next. Where would he sleep? Where did he take cover when it rained?

"Thanks for your time. Never give up!" he said. "Rely on God!" He smiled and rolled away on his shopping cart.

Lucas reminded me of the pure goodness in life even in the midst of tough circumstances. And if Lucas, with all the difficulties he faced each day, never gave up, how could I? I was grateful for food, shelter, and this job, this crazy gig on the Bering Sea. Lucas's words fed me with resolve in the moment. It's during the hardest times in life when we gain the most strength to go on. If we can only endure.

I knew if this ship sank, the chance of survival was low. Without a survival suit, I'd be hypothermic. My limbs would become numb and I'd be unable to tread water. Death by drowning in five minutes. With a suit, I'd last thirty minutes to possibly hours in calm seas, without the usual twenty-foot-high waves breaking overhead.

A seasoned Coast Guard pilot told me, "If your ship goes down, stay with another person. If you find yourself struggling out there alone, you'll likely turn over and allow yourself to die. In the end, it is your own will that keeps you alive." Some of us—I—would fight to the end.

My mom said, "Quitters never win and winners never quit." But I remember the one time she gave up.

I was in second grade, my brother and I still shared bunk beds in our third-floor apartment on the south side of Chicago. It was on a noisy stretch of Pulaski Street, between White Castle and the Tasty Freeze where we'd walk from Grandma's to buy swirl cones. There was no swamp or backyard to play in, no trees for us to climb, and no dad around to build play things for us. We could cross the busy street to the park or lay on the hot sidewalk and watch the lines of ants, with no shelter of delicate peonies to crawl into, pass through the cracks.

My brother and I usually went everywhere together, but I stayed at Grandma's more. Gram said, "It's too much with both of you here. Tommy is a handful." I thought all boys were handfuls. She slept with her blood-clot prone legs elevated on a wedge pillow and a rosary under her head. She kept a wrinkled paper sac full of prescription pills within arm's reach to treat conditions I couldn't pronounce, like diverticulitis. There was no rough-housing allowed on her hard, straight-backed, red velvet furniture. I thought her pink flowered china, with the gold rims, belonged in a palace, not in a two-bedroom brick house behind overgrown bushes and a pine tree that covered the windows.

Mom called Gram a "Prima Donna," but she was a beautiful, Hollywood movie star to me. She used proper words like "darling," "bosom," and "masticate," and called me "Dearest Chickie." She curled her long white hair at the bottom and tucked in the top with a jeweled comb. She wore mink stoles in the winter and fancy hats in the summer. The hats, some with tags still on them, were kept in boxes that she stuffed in the closet and smelled of mothballs. She sketched arched brows over her sparkly blue eyes and wore bright orange lipstick that left a ring around her Kent cigarettes. She wore her nails painted, usually Corvette red. "Don't you point at me with that claw!" Mom screamed at Gram when they fought. That's the way it was in our family.

Gram often told me, "Laura, I'm on a limited budget," as she swiped the square jellies and ketchup packets from restaurant tables, because buying a full jar was wasteful. I admired her use of one paper towel, rinsed and air-dried three times before it could go in the garbage: first your hands, then the counter, then the floor.

I loved Gram, and I knew Mom did, too, even if they didn't get along much of the time. Even if it was true that Gram refused to change my mom's diapers when she was a baby. Supposedly she waited until her husband, Tommy, came home to change them for her. Maybe Mom wound up loving him more than Gram because of it.

I remember the night the trucks with the red flashing lights and high-pitched alarms came to our south Chicago apartment, because I'd taken a handful of eggs from the refrigerator and put them into a box of rags under my bunk bed. I pointed a reading light on it to keep them safe and warm, just like a mama chicken would do. I wanted to save those baby chickies. Tom was tucked in his bunk above me, and our Siamese cat Mae Lee was circling, meowing, and acting scared. I prayed and prayed in my bunk, "Please God, make everything okay."

Curious about the reason for the sirens and lights, Tom and I went to Mom's bedroom, standing outside the doorway holding hands. The room filled with people: Grandma, her boyfriend, my Aunt Irene, my cousins, the paramedics. No one told us to go back to bed this time.

Mom was lying in her big bed with her mouth open, more tired than I'd ever seen her. The phone, off the hook, was hanging by the twisted cord. Maybe she'd called to fight with Grandma or Daddy? The paramedics picked her up and put her on a narrow, rollaway bed. It was taller than me, so I couldn't see her.

Tommy asked, "Why are they hauling Mommy away?"

"I guess she's really sick," I answered. "They called it a nervous breakdown. Whatever that means."

"Yeah, that's probably why she had to take so many pills," he said, wiping his teary eyes.

Pills dotted the bed and scattered on the shag carpet. Mom didn't keep her pills in a wrinkled paper lunch sack like Grandma.

Tommy didn't know it then, but I did. Mom wanted to die that night. She rolled over into a dark abyss, alone in despair, like a man overboard in the icy Bering Sea. Without someone by her side, she quit fighting. She would've allowed herself to die. It wouldn't be the last time.

Several months later, we learned that Mom and Dad were divorcing. It wasn't until I was a preteen that I asked Mom, "Why did you get divorced?"

"I was tired of being your father's punching bag," she said.

We had a plastic, blowup punching bag with a scary clown face on it. Mom would say, "If you want to hit someone, don't hit each other; box the clown." The clown would wobble, go down, and pop right back up. That didn't usually happen when you hit a person.

Mom said Daddy wanted to take my brother away and split us, and our bunk beds, up like a litter of Mae Lee's kittens. I wished we could've all stayed together. Happily? Ever? What comes after?

He lived an hour away with a department store sales clerk who sported fancy shoes, a red curly afro, and long fake eyelashes that looked like tarantulas. Her oldest son stayed in his room and sucked smoke from a gurgling pipe with a glass chimney. There wasn't room for us in his apartment. When we visited Dad on the weekends, Tom and I slept on blue foldout cots in his living room, side by side in our matching Barnum & Bailey Circus sleeping bags. He made our favorite foods—macaroni and cheese and homemade pumpkin pies—and let us pick out our own boxes of sugar-coated Cocoa Puffs and Captain Crunch from the bottom shelves, off limits under Mom's watch.

Dad had changed though. His eyes lost their twinkle, and he didn't play his records and sing Elvis songs much anymore.

After the ambulances came and took Mom, we stayed with Dad until she got better. I didn't want to move again and have to change schools. Plus, cots are comfortable for a weekend, but not for much longer, kinda like the rack I found myself sleeping in now.

I laid in my bunk, sloshing side to side like a slippery fish in my sample basket. I would never forget the rip-roar of a squall, lying at the mercy of nature, pressed to the edge, where danger meets death, or seeing my mother give up on her own life.

I was learning to navigate this fragile gift of life. I knew that problems would come wave after wave and without warning. Sometimes in light gusts; sometimes as a full-on hurricane. The sea was teaching me to ride out the rough spots, to believe a better day was on the horizon, and to never give up, like Lucas. I wouldn't give up on surviving, the pursuit of my dreams, or the possibility of finding love. Good things would find me, even at sea.

After a few interrupted hours of sleep, I awoke the next morning feeling better and less fearful. This job, this ship, was my saving grace and the sole reason for my existence right now. It had given me a spark of hope, for financial security and a path to my future. Sometimes that's all we need. Trough and crest. Day and night. I was discovering my resilience with each passing storm. A storm may last for days on the Bering Sea, but in a family it could last for years.

10

~~~~~

SISTER SHIP

THE honeymoon period was clearly over, and the weeks dragged on. I hadn't given much thought to how it would feel to be out of touch with land life for a month or more at a time. When else would a single woman lock herself up with twenty-five men in tight quarters for three months and be unable to get away from them except for maybe a day or two?

The Bering Sea, I discovered, is where life presses pause while everyone else's plays forward on land. I was learning to live there, too, in the pauses, between steps and held breaths and crashing waves. My focus shifted, at least for a while, from worrying about a long-term and uncertain future to the more immediate challenges of each day. I slowly let loose of time and all I'd left behind.

On land, most of us count down time by the number of work-days remaining until the weekend. "It's hump day. Only two more days 'til Friday." At sea, we worked around the clock with no days off. No weekends. No holidays. Each day, each week, held equal weight. "Oh, it's your birthday? Happy Birthday. Now get back to work." Instead, time was marked by "How many days have we been out here?"; "How full is the freezer with product?"; "How much fuel remains in the tank?"; and "How many days until we hit port?" When I started this trip, I didn't know the answer to that last burning question would be "Over a month."

After a month straight at sea with no land in sight, I felt deprived from all angles. I lacked solid sleep. Unable to exchange stories, or rant or rave by phone, I craved empathy from friends. I wrote letters almost daily, pouring my heart onto the page, only to watch them pile up in my duffle bag, wrinkle, and fray. The guys joked, "Oh, we can send your letters when we get to the mail buoy." An at-sea, old-time pony express? I wanted to believe it was true, but like a Midwestern fool's errand of snipe-hunting, it was just another falsehood.

I desired to watch a current sitcom, hear a new song on the radio, or even hear an actual weather report, one that didn't come in by a weather fax, for any area that wasn't the Bering Sea. With no live or breaking news broadcasts, I often wondered, "What the heck is going on in the world? It was a good day when we got buzzed by a Coast Guard plane or we spotted another vessel with our binoculars, just a dot on the horizon. A reminder that someone else was out there.

My taste buds, too, grew ravenous for what I couldn't get: the crisp crunch of fresh fruits and vegetables; a simple can of soda; a favorite chocolate treat; a foamy, piping hot hazelnut steamer or latte; or a perfectly grilled killer cheeseburger with extra everything on top. I wished I could simply walk or jog for miles on ground that didn't shift beneath my feet. I missed all these things.

What I didn't expect after a month at sea was the isolation I'd feel. Surely I'd lose my mind if the only one waiting for my words was the next page of my journal, a rumpled letter, or a giant cod puppet. What I desperately yearned for, above all, was companionship.

Granted, I had the ear of Captain Gabe. I enjoyed his playful company, it was like spending time with a brother's best friend. You were attracted to him, but you couldn't date him because doing so would disrupt the natural order. And though his comments, such as, "I know how to fix that neck pain," or "I know you dig taller men, but I can wear platforms," teetered on the edge of flirtation, he was committed to his girlfriend back home. Plus his California lingo was enough to keep us in the "just friends" category for a lifetime. Nonetheless, after a month at sea, the chair in the wheel-house, from which I enjoyed Captain Gabe's company, became my refuge. Except for the occasional surprise.

I'd trotted up to the wheelhouse for a break between hauls. As soon as I entered, Captain Gabe's eyebrows headed toward the ceiling and his mouth twisted. I often saw the same expression on the face of my little brother—in trouble again, cheeks flushed with guilt. He was talking over the VHF radio with another captain, a partner and competitor, but all calls over this radio were transmitted to every boat in the fleet.

The voice of the other captain came over the speaker, "Yeah, Gabe, my observer here says you're one lucky guy right now. Is your observer as beautiful as he says?"

The unnamed observer must have remembered me from training in Seattle.

Gabe playfully winked at me as if to say, "Let's see where this goes." In response to the other captain, he said, "Yeah, Dude. She's a *fo-ox* alright. I get the good looking observers and you get the fat, old men."

I wasn't sure if I should smile or punch him, but I took it as a compliment. After all, I wasn't feeling very foxy in my baggy sweats, turtleneck, and plaid flannel and could use a little admiration. I'd become immune to fish scales and wipe-away-with-your-shirt-sleeve slime on my face. I looked my worst. Anything remotely girly—a scoop neck T-shirt, perfume, makeup, or a flash of painted toenails—would attract the men in blind navigation toward me like moths to the light.

The voice on the other end continued, "I'm holding up a sexy, long-legged centerfold right now. My observer said your observer is her twin. I'd like to . . ."

My face crumpled into shock. I sucker-punched Gabe's arm and ripped away the radio handset. I pressed the button and blasted Captain Hot-n-Bothered, "I'll show you her twin!"

A long pause was followed by a stuttered, "I . . . I'm sorry. I didn't know you were listening." *Everyone,* the whole fleet, was listening. He signed off in seconds, and silence echoed across the Bering Sea; there wasn't even the sound of static.

Unable to form a reasonable defense in his head, Captain Gabe held his hand out, ready for me to slap it with a ruler. "That was fun." he said, smiling. "See, what did I tell you? All men *are* pigs."

I didn't believe so, but "All men are pigs" had been his mantra to me daily since I boarded. I knew the captain had set the guy up and was being playful. But there's an element of truth behind every joke. How could I let my guard down and trust the others?

Frustrated, I sighed, "I miss women. I want my mom." Even I was surprised by my reaction—Mom wasn't the one I typically turned to when I needed support. But I was starving for a familiar voice I could trust and a female viewpoint. Before email and a cell phone in everyone's pocket, extended trips made it impossible to stay in close contact with family and friends. Traditional communications by snail mail would have to wait for our return to Dutch Harbor to offload. After a month at sea, I still had not yet touched down in port. I was allowed to send and receive limited fax messages from the ship, but the going rate of ten dollars per minute to send one double-spaced, handwritten page was too expensive. Ten bucks was three times the minimum hourly wage at the time. Plus, most people didn't have access to a fax machine. The copy shop would receive my fax, probably read it for entertainment, and call the intended recipient's phone number written on the cover page.

That person would have to go to the nearest copy shop to pay for and pick up my letter. The onboard satellite phone was unreliable and also a pricey fifteen bucks per minute. I couldn't afford to take a deep breath at that rate, and I had no way to give my family "the signal."

The signal was designed by my mom and grandma before the advent of answering machines, voicemail, and caller ID. My brother and I used it our entire childhood. Mom would drop us off at the roller rink, the Boys and Girls Club, the bowling alley, or a movie theater. She would say, "When you're done and ready for me to pick you up, give me the signal."

When the time came, we would drop a dime into a payphone, let the phone ring twice, and hang up. We'd get the dime back and repeat the process. Again, Mom wouldn't answer. That was the signal for her to pick us up. We didn't waste ten cents, and we could use the same dime over and over.

If we didn't have a dime, we had a way around that, too. We'd dial zero and wait for the operator to answer, "Hello. You've reached the operator. How can I help you?"

"Operator, I need to make a collect call," I'd say, and then give her our home number.

Mom would pick up after the third ring (never by the second), and the operator would ask, "Ma'am, we have a collect call from Laura. Do you accept the charges?"

"No. I won't accept the charges," Mom replied before hanging up. A different signal, but again, no charge.

I couldn't use those tricks on the ship to save ten dollars a minute instead of a dime, but it was payback time. Captain Gabe, struck with a wave of conscience, asked me, "Would you like to talk to your mother? We're in a good spot to call on the VHF radio through a marine operator out of St. Paul Island. It's free for you today."

The opportunity to use the radio was a rare blessing. Surprisingly, he reached my mom in Missouri. "Hello," he said. "Is this Laura's mom? Hold on. I have your daughter here." All the tension was gone when he winked and passed me the radio.

I grabbed the handset, smirked, and squinted my eyes at him. "Now go pray for forgiveness," I said.

Hanging onto the chart table for balance against the rolls of the boat, I cheered, "Hi, Mom. I can't talk long. Everything we say is broadcasted over the radio to anyone listening." I sneered at Gabe. "I just wanted to say hello and tell you I'm okay." I would've said that regardless, no matter what had happened. I sounded strong, but secretly I needed to hear her voice.

She sounded fearful, as if I had been kidnapped and this was the call for ransom money. "What's that noise? I can't hear you very well," she shouted. "Are you off the boat yet? Where are you?" The five-second delays between speakers broke the conversation into awkward pauses. Each of us attempted to not talk over the other, which Mom did regularly. How sad I'd be to lose our connection.

"I'm still on the ship," I said, slow and clear. "It's pretty incredible out here, though the weather has been rough. At least the captain is great." I shot lasers at him with my eyes. Waves poured over the bow and splashed up the sides of the second-story wheelhouse. "I have no idea when I'll be back in town, but I'll call as soon as we hit port." We might be out here another month. Or more.

Mom's voice shifted to unusually soft and concerned, "I don't like you being out there, Laura."

Was she really worried, or just concerned I wasn't there for her whenever she needed me? The tables had turned since my childhood. Usually, it was me who advised and consoled her. Mom called me to cry, to dump her ails on me, and spill over with emotion like breakers at high tide over a shallow beach. The family joke was you could put the phone down, come back ten minutes later, and she'd still be talking. She talked at us, not with us. And usually the topic was her.

After high school ended and I moved out, she stopped listening. Maybe she never listened, and I just began to notice it when I needed someone—her—most. She took my gain of independence as rejection, somehow as a cue to stop mothering. I turned to nature when I needed nurture. On this call, with our feet firmly planted in two different worlds, she heard every word. For the first time since I was a teenager, she didn't rattle on with a list of complaints, and I felt consoled by her.

I wanted to tell her about my new life: the towering waves, us cutting through sheets of ice, the wide-ranging cast of characters aboard, the unbelievable amounts of huge fish, the fact I hadn't seen land since I'd left almost a month ago, and my loneliness being apart from family and friends. But I didn't. The stronger I sounded, the stronger I'd feel, and the less she'd worry.

I assured her, "I'm fine, Mom. I've got twenty-five men out here to protect me."

"That's what I'm afraid of." Her voice cracked. I didn't tell her about Underwear Man and my other male roommates, or my "anchor time" crush on Russell, or the constant competition for my attention. She only needed to know I was doing well and enjoying my Bering Sea adventure.

Captain Gabe stood next to me and prodded, "Tell her about my metal-hook limb and eye patch." I shook my head sideways to brush him off. I wished he was anywhere but the wheelhouse. But perhaps a minute of privacy would shatter my tough shell and everyone—my mom, the marine operator, Captain Hot-n-Bothered, who was probably listening, and the entire fishing fleet—would hear me break down and cry.

The reception began to crackle. "I have to go, Mom. I love you." I hated to hang up so soon. Though I was unable to talk to

Walter or my brother, for a bright moment I had connected with land and time ticked forward.

"Be safe," she said. "I love you." I needed to hear those last three words at the end of every conversation. They always sounded so final, as if she'd be carried off in an ambulance and I'd never be able to say, "I love you, too" again.

I wanted to tell Mom so much more, and for her to hear me. Captain Gabe apparently did too, so he slipped into his stateroom that evening and composed a letter to her. I was curious about what he'd written and how much, if any of it, was true. Later, at times he'd say, "Oh, *this* is going in my letter to your mom!" It would be another month before I'd know its contents.

Still feeling like the outsider, I needed to hear someone cared about me out here on my Alaskan adventure. Or at least to hear from someone who could relate to my experience as a woman, like maybe Stef. The call to my mom temporarily fed my need for female companionship, but it wasn't near enough. The next opportunity came weeks later in the form of a crisis, only one of the many I would witness on this ship.

"Oh, no! We're caught on another ship's gear! Back it down!" yelled Dean, holding a Victorinox deck knife.

"We've got a 700-pound sleeper shark wound up in the tow!" Larone yelled with a slow drawl up through the hatch to Captain Gabe in the wheelhouse. "Man, this is f'd up! Do we part the line or hack its tail off?" Its massive body hung outside the hatch, still alive, but drowning, tangled in snarled loops. I couldn't watch. I might pass out.

"Grab an extinguisher and follow me!" Jazz yelled to the engineer. "The clothes dryer is on fire!"

"Quick!" Ed said. "The greenhorn has a hook through his hand! Huh, huh, huh." Several crewmen dropped their duties to assist.

"We'll have to put a temporary filling in Russell's tooth until we get back to port," said Hobey, probably wanting to rub some magic herbal concoction on it, too. Was there a travel kit for that? Would they pack it with cotton and a wad of gum and tell him to suck up and deal with it for another month?

"One of the guys claims to have a cockroach stuck in his ear," said the chief engineer. Further investigation revealed the crewman really *did* have a dead cockroach in his ear canal.

Unlike the other crises, I hoped this next one was news of salvation. Word spread fast through the vessel, "We're out of toilet paper!"

What? Yes, it's true! After forty-two days at sea, we ran out of toilet paper *and* packaging material, also called fiber. We had nothing to wipe with. Ah, but this emergency could be a Godsend, our way back into port. I would soon walk on sweet, solid earth, send and receive mail, talk on a real phone, possibly eat in a civilized restaurant or shop in a store; and maybe even see my new best friend, Stef. The horns shall blow and the balloons and confetti shall fall from the sky like New Year's Eve. Snow day. School's closed. Pop some bubbly. It was time to celebrate.

Wrong, naïve Observer Girl!

We had copious fuel and were nowhere near full freezer capacity. No, thanks to the Seattle office and Captain Gabe, who found a different way to restock our paper products, we were deprived of our chance to return to port. Instead, our sister ship, having already departed out of Dutch, was on its way to deliver supplies to us, here, at sea. My hopeful plan had been foiled. It's not a snow day after all, you do have to go to school, and, bonus, there's homework.

Sister ships are managed or owned by the same company. Though competition is high between them, crews and captains share a team mentality, typically work on either vessel, and, like sisters, help each other in times of crises—like during a toilet paper shortage. Disappointed we weren't headed back to town and busting at the chance to get off my vessel for any length of time, I watched as our sister ship sailed toward us.

As the vessel edged nearer, I spotted someone on deck. What's this, a sister ship delivering a *sister*? Starved for an ounce of real-life female company, I was prepared to perform whatever stunt was required to get off this ship. I would become the human cannonball and be fired to the other vessel or tied to a buoy and floated over. I needed a change of scenery, to walk steps I hadn't taken every day for over a month, and to commiserate with another woman, face-to-face.

The ships tied up side by side in the swell, separated by giant buoys that absorbed the harsh swipes of metal on metal. Their deck boss invited me aboard. The boats were too far apart and the crossing too risky to long jump as I did at the dock on my first day. I wasn't going down a swaying Jacob's ladder, and I wasn't up for drowning and being sandwiched between two ships. It was decided. The hoist method. They wrapped me up in a webbed cargo net like freight and transferred me to their deck by a crane in exchange for cases of toilet paper and fiber. This was a fun, at-sea amusement ride. This was newsworthy. I felt like Keiko the orca being released after being held captive in a shallow pool for months.

The stocky, square-chinned observer approached me with a firm handshake and a stiff crack of a smile. She, too, was the only female aboard her ship. Would we trade stories, books, and magazines or scented lotion? Immediately, the red warning flags went up. The summary of her stay veered negative: the work was awful, the food was bad, the guys were evil, and the captain was a jerk. As we toured her vessel and strolled past staterooms, her anger built with shotgun criticisms of each crewman, reasons left unsaid. Was her experience and perspective that different from mine? She'd been out a month longer than me, and she'd been off the boat at least once in Dutch Harbor. Is she what I'd soon become after another two months at sea?

In her eyes, she was treated poorly. Was she mistreated, or was she just difficult to work alongside? I didn't know, so I said, "I hope you can go home soon. It's hard being out here for so long." We needed the same reassurances and condolences. She had a partner back in Seattle, but she reminded me of how alone I'd felt there, too. Except for my mom, Tom, and Walter, did anyone *really* miss me? Maybe a few friends scattered through the US? Did Luke, who was likely lounging poolside under the hot Florida sun? Maybe Stef, bucking this same ocean as me. Feeling quite the opposite of uplifted, I realized that the neglected houseplants in my efficiency apartment probably missed me most. They were all I had waiting for me back in Seattle.

After a brief half hour the crane operator signaled me for liftoff. He handed me a bag of mail for the crew that had been stacking up at the office in Dutch. There would be none for me, as my mail went not to the mail buoy or the ship's office, but to the observer bunkhouse. Until I reached port, my life at sea would remain on pause until I could hit land and press play again.

I had a need to mutually commiserate, to exchange stories with another female who possibly understood daily life out here. Instead of being enriched and strengthened by girl power, I left disheartened. No refreshing conversation or relief was found with this other sister. Gender didn't unite this time. I was far from port and out of luck, but deep in a shipload of toilet paper—enough to get us through our last days, or weeks, of our first lengthy trip at sea.

11

DANGER

WHEN the weather gets rough, a choice has to be made: keep fishing in an attempt to make more money; find shelter leeward of an island and wait it out; or, in this case, pull the gear and haul our butts right through the storm. We aimed for new fishing grounds in the eastern Bering Sea. It was early May; temperatures hovered around thirty degrees Fahrenheit. Steam days, or travel days, were usually free days for me, allowing me to catch up on my data, sleep, journaling, or reading. However, on this day the winds were blowing a roaring fifty knots (near sixty mph), and the seas broke at a solid twenty-five feet. We slogged through snow falling like fist-sized wads of wet tissue. The amount of snow and polar freeze should taper off by the end of the month, but for now the weather was predicted to get worse before it got better.

I felt conflicted about being in the wheelhouse in this kind of weather. Standing eye-level with two-story walls of waves, I wondered if they'd blow out the wheelhouse windows. My muscles tensed as I awaited each crash over us. There, from deep inside the pulsing heart of the wave, I begged God to lift up our bow, to pop us up again and again. I fearfully anticipated the smack of another, maybe a rogue wave, the big daddy of all that hits unexpectedly between the regular combers. We rode out the aftershock of this earthquake of a storm. I wanted to be on the bridge to read the captain's face and be comforted by his sea sense, but I didn't want him to see the fear in mine.

Every external surface on the windward side of the boat—the gear, windows, hydraulics, buoys, and railings—were covered with icicles hanging like stalactites. The crew paired up for safety and took one-hour shifts on deck with mallets and baseball bats to break up the frozen layers. When the ice got too thick on one side, the captain angled the ship to let ice build on the other side, like ballast, to keep the boat balanced. We had all heard the nightmares of vessels that "turtled"—too heavy on one side so they flipped over and, like a turtle, were unable to right themselves—in storms like these. We plowed into the waves, but with each turn we battled the deep troughs with a lopsided swing. Mother Nature was giving us a beating. This was no day of rest.

By evening the weather had worsened. "Snacky Cakes," Captain Gabe stated, "You're gonna have to hang on. Winds are gnarly, upwards of sixty-five knots. The waves are increasing. Probably over thirty-five feet high now, some of the largest out here. Welcome to hell."

I'd already seen waves of breathtaking beauty and docile as a summer breeze, but this night we met the beast of nature. Hurricane-force winds. A storm rarely experienced on land. Bad weather seemed more severe at night, but this evening it felt evil, as if ghastly spirits were whirling around, penetrating the air. Storm clouds blanked out the stars and moon. The gantry lights casted a dim glow on the frozen metal deck and the dark slate ocean. Ice continued to cover the vessel, transforming it into a top-heavy floating igloo. I was too nervous to be seasick. Others weren't so lucky.

Captain Gabe set the propeller at an 80 percent pitch and we plugged away at a sluggish two to three knots just to maintain our position against the blow. If we ran any harder, the red engine temperature light flashed its warning. Then . . . BAM! I closed my eyes and squeezed whatever I could hold onto. The whole boat shook, and we were completely engulfed by green water. We were *in* the waves more than we were on top of them. Our wake stirred black with angry, white-tipped foam caps. Even the gulls were absent now. There was no reprieve for us, no hiding in the safety of a cove or behind an island. Instead, we turned the other cheek and got busted in the chops. Over and over again.

Engine checks ran around the clock, but tonight an alarm sounded. Unlike the chirp of a smoke detector signaling it's time to change the battery, alarms mean serious trouble on a fishing boat. If there was a problem, a Coast Guard ship, our only hope for rescue, was nowhere in sight, and since only one or two roamed this giant ocean at one time, it was possible they were days away.

I hoped the alarm wasn't signaling a Freon or ammonia leak in the refrigeration system. Both gases are dangerous and deadly. Freon is a scentless and colorless gas. An ultraviolet dye is pumped into the system so the leaks can be detected with a special bulb. Heavier than air, Freon displaces oxygen in small, enclosed areas and replaces the air in your lungs. By the time you inhale it, it may already be too late. First your vision blurs, and then you suffocate. Ammonia reacts with air to form a caustic substance, corrosive to any exposed skin, eyes, nose, and throat. The possibility of any such leaks aboard scared me. Word was out that an engineer on another boat had recently died from a Freon leak.

I was overly familiar with freak accidents. In 1978, I was ten years old. We had moved from the south side of Chicago to West Chicago, to be closer to Mom's new beau Walter, and back to Cicero. Mom was attending cosmetology school during the day and bartending at night for an older Greek man. Neighborhood taverns were everywhere in Chicago in the '70s. We just happened to live on the corner attached to one. At both bars, the regulars flipped quarters to my brother and me from their stools. We'd pump them into games like air hockey, foosball, and pinball, or we'd feed the jukebox. Sometimes we'd combine our quarters to buy a frozen Tombstone sausage pizza for two dollars. At the corner table under the dim lights we'd do our homework and drink Shirley Temples with extra cherries and an umbrella, special like Mom made for us.

At the time, I was learning to cook and wanted to do it all by myself—I had burns on my fingers and arms to prove it. I'd make entire meals from scratch, such as meatloaf, green beans, and mashed potatoes, or hot coffee for Mom and chocolate cookies. My brother and I finally had separate rooms and got to choose our own wallpaper: a *Star Wars* theme in silver, blues, and reds for Tom; lemon yellow with green and white tulips for me. This apartment behind the bar became another blip on our list of moves, but the time there changed all of our lives forever.

Walter came around more. He had hazel eyes, a bald head, and a giant, smelly stogy always hanging from his buck teeth. Grandma didn't like Walter calling her "Ma." She'd scold him, "You are older than me. Don't you call me that."

Walter told us of his childhood adventures during The Depression and the Prohibition era, when people went without. He'd hopped coal trains behind his house, swept piles of it onto the tracks, retrieved it with a wheelbarrow, and pushed it home to fuel their stove. His mom chased down chickens on the road with the car, because if you hit one you could eat it. And it seemed everyone was in the trade of illegal moonshine.

He brought us our favorite treats: Swedish Fish, Dunkin' Donuts, and coffee cakes from the Polish bakery. Sometimes he'd bring us cool stuff from his Italian buddy's pawn shop in downtown Chicago, things we never had: a good color television that you didn't need pliers to change the channel or wrap aluminum foil around the antenna; a VCR; and appliances like a microwave, The Hot Dogger, or a popcorn machine. Mom liked his gifts, too, and called them "hot," which to me meant a hot deal, but I later learned it meant that it was likely they had been stolen and hocked for quick cash.

I loved everything about Walter, except that he wasn't yet fully divorced from his wife. I wished he was my second dad, because then he could live with us all the time. Plus, his adopted daughter, Margaret—four years older than me, a high school freshman with curly blonde hair and perfect white teeth, who smacked her watermelon Bubble Yum and snorted when she laughed—would be my sister.

It was the end of summer break, Labor Day, the day before I would enter fifth grade. At Walter's house, barbecued chicken and hotdogs were on the grill, sprinklers and squirt guns kept us cool, and a huge trampoline and games galore entertained us. The highlight was Margaret's go-kart, though she was with her mom that weekend. We zipped around the circular driveway like Mario Andretti. Tom and the three kids who lived in the tiny studio apartment beside us cheered me on from the sidelines, eager for their turn. Smiling, with a face full of crooked teeth, my long brown hair swirling behind me in the summer wind, I shouted with each lap as I passed them, "Eat my dust!"

Without warning, my head wrenched back, hard against the padded seat back; I fumbled to brake and bring the kart to a halt. "Owww, my head. My neck!" What was happening? The engine continued to race. Above it and my own yelling, I heard screams of horror, most prominent the cry of my little brother. I felt the burn, the sting, the unbearable torture. My hair had become entangled in the fan belt, and the exposed engine wound and pulled and peeled my scalp from my skull, like the rind from an orange. Warm blood pulsed out to meet cool air. My mother catapulted from the house shouting, "Oh, my God! Look at all the blood! My BABY!" My eyes closed and my languid body listed, falling into the shadows.

Peace somehow replaced the excruciating pain as Kim, a family friend and a nurse, placed a cool, wet towel on my sweaty forehead.

"How's Tommy?" I asked. "Where's my brother?" I heard his cries in the background. "Is he okay?"

"Yes. He's okay," she said. "He's just worried about you." Mom, hysterical, was kept at a distance.

I felt the blood drain from my head, and a feathery lightness lifting from my body. I knew I would soon be with Great-grandpa Joe and my two goldfish; I'd finally get to meet Mom's dad and Elvis in heaven.

Sound amplified and the darkness beneath my closed lids turned to light.

"I'm going to die, aren't I?" I murmured.

"No, Honey, you're not going to die," Kim said. "You're going to be fine. Be strong."

I didn't believe her, though the throbbing stopped momentarily. All went numb.

I heard the sirens. The ambulance was coming to save me, but by then I'd lost all sense. Nothing made sense. Why was this happening? A fog encircled me as they pried my head loose from the gnawing, hungry metal of the engine. The paramedics wrapped my head in a wet turban, hoisted me onto a gurney, shoved me into the ambulance, and closed the door, like a cake into an Easy-Bake oven. Mom was not allowed to ride with me. I faded in and out of awareness, encouraged by the ambulance's high speed as it ran through red lights, but frowning at the pain and blaring shriek of the sirens. Since that day, I pray whenever I hear a siren—for God to ease someone else's pain.

At the hospital, a shiny pair of scissors cut away my favorite blue and white gingham shirt. People in white shirts surrounded me, their gloved hands moving quickly, but I couldn't understand their muffled voices. Silent darkness followed. Life hit pause.

When I awoke from surgery, I discovered that I had lost three-quarters of my scalp and with it hair that would never grow back in place of scar tissue. I also found a new injury I hadn't expected on my right hip. The doctors had removed a rectangular skin graft, about the size of a standard envelope, and stitched it to my head to replace my lost scalp.

The wound on my hip puffed, oozed, and burned like a giant blister for a month. Each day as I healed, we'd wash my wounds, blow them dry, apply ointment, and change the dressings.

After the accident, I wanted to skip school and avoid being seen in public. I felt like a freak show and constantly wondered if all people could see was my ugliness, my exposed scars. The phrase, *"Is it covered?"* consumed my thoughts. The words were entrenched in my mind, except when I wore a hat or when I slept, though the words often invaded my dreams. Now, along with "Brace Face" and "Train tracks," the kids at school called me "Kojak," "Baldy sour," "Skin head," and "Lollipop." My Italian boy crush now liked a different girl, one with pretty hair. "Sticks and stones may break your bones. . ." Mom reassured me. "Laurie girl, you're still the same beautiful person inside and out. If kids make fun of you, they weren't your friends in the first place." If they kept it up, I might have to fight them.

The dying leaves, ochre and rust, blew off trees, while I looked out of season, out of place, and outdated. I now wore head scarves, babushkas, like the old Polish grandmas, to cover my bare scalp when scarves were uncool and so '60s. While everyone else was wearing tight, peg-leg Jordache and Gloria Vanderbilt jeans with rhinestones on the pockets, I had to wear lightweight skirts that wouldn't aggravate my sensitive hip, still covered with gauze. No fifth-grader would be caught dead wearing a milkmaid outfit, except maybe as a costume for Halloween. This was not "The Jordache Look." I tried to keep perspective, as much as a ten-year-old is capable of anyway. I told myself, "At least I'm better off than the kids in the burn ward at the hospital." Some lost half their bodies. In the hospital, I had heard their cries in the middle of the night. Mom reminded me, "Laurie, at least the scar isn't on your pretty little face." It was months before I could bare to look at my own scar in the mirror. As I cried, I kept thinking, "It could've been worse."

Now I knew how my brother felt, being teased because he was a little different. We could now be tormented together, both of us with our hidden head injuries. Tom's problem couldn't be mended by doctors. My surgeries resumed every ten months for seven years. Each time the doctors cut out a piece of the scar tissue on my scalp and pulled and tightened it like a drum skin. Later, Mom impressed upon me any positives that could come from this atrocity: "Well, you'll never need a facelift when you're Grandma's age." When you'd rather cry, sometimes it's best to accept your circumstances and try to laugh.

The doctors reduced, but could never remove the entire wound. Each year I'd change up my hairdo to accommodate the slightly smaller scar. I'd spend the rest of my life under duress on windy days. I'd never be caught without a hair tie, and I'm still thankful the basic ponytail hasn't gone out of style. Getting my hair wet at the pool or beach stressed me equally. And there would always be the bumpy scar on my transformed hip boldly showing below the leg line of any bathing suit. These scars are a daily reminder of how life can change with one shift of the wind or one lap around a track.

And now, with possible Freon or ammonia leaks and tumultuous weather, the danger level was high. It seemed a freak accident was always near. I feared for my life with each slam of the bow.

The storms made me feel small, dispensable, and filled me with a deep respect that edged on fear. But why should I be afraid? The guys did this all the time, right? The next day we charged forward with a burst of adrenaline; each day was a ride on a different roller coaster. Today's ride was powered by thirty-knot winds and fifteen-foot-high waves.

The guys hated non-fishing days, because they were paid in crew shares when the stakes went up, and the more fish they caught, the more they profited. I, however, got paid the same.

We were at the end of one set, which I passed on sampling, and the guys were prepping for the next. I told myself this was just another normal rough weather day of bouncing between railings, walls, and equipment.

There's safety in numbers. I stood in the rear of the vessel, where the slacktaker pulls the empty groundline returned from fore to aft. The gear overhaul work area looked like a torture chamber. Here the gangions were unwound and recoiled, with each hook separated and slid into "magazine" storage racks, ready for the next set. The area was less exposed, and I could stand tall with the collective strength of six men. Their confidence gave me courage in the storms. I braced myself between two crewmen to help repair damaged hooks and gangions. The hanging coils of line swayed from side to side, along with Tito's (one of the Samoans) long ponytails—I was pretty sure it would someday be wrapped around or yanked by some hook, line, fan, or conveyor belt.

The boom box blasted MC Hammer's "You Can't Touch This," a distraction from the weather. Russell, as usual, bobbed his knees and wiggled his upper body sideways to the beat. Larone said to him, "Man, Rico Suave, you call that dancing? That ain't even the 'cabbage patch.'" Russell kept working his subtle moves despite the ribbing. Whenever a cool groove played we'd say, "Hey Russell, dance for us." He'd dip and sway, slow and controlled. Not exactly dancing, but entertaining.

Dean, with his scraggly beard, backwards hat, and gray sweatshirt stained with fish guts, became more attractive and endearing to me as our trip went on. But today he puffed on his cigarette with a scowl as he loaded magazine racks in preparation for a set and snapped weights and floats onto the line. Referring to his lack of direction in life as much as the bad weather, he grumbled, "Why the hell are we out here doing this?" Sometimes my thoughts echoed his. The long trips took its toll on our attitudes. We all needed a break from work. From the vessel. We needed port.

Next to me stood Daniel, a five-foot-three Irishman with tightly wound red hair stuffed under a striped stocking cap. I'd already been demoted to his D-list. Weeks earlier, when I saw him pop up through a man hatch in the aft deck floor, I made the mistake of saying, "Hey, Daniel, you look like a leprechaun." The words just came out. I apologized, but he'd heard it one time too many times. He might not have forgiven me, but he put up with me because I liked to talk fishing and he loved to share his knowledge.

We were getting ready to set two parallel lines more than 200 fathoms deep. Daniel explained in his swingy, Irish accent, "The fathom originates back when fishermen determined depth by dropping weighted sounding lines. The average arm span was six feet long. One fathom." It was no time for a short joke, but no way did Daniel's arms span six feet.

Soon, the line would zip through the auto baiter at four hooks per second, jetting out from the stern almost 15,000 squid-baited hooks per line. Seagulls and fulmars flocked behind the vessel, ready to dive-bomb the fast-sinking gear. Sometimes dead, water-logged birds came up on the line during a haulback, and I counted them as part of my sample. While tying gangions and swaying to the waves, I watched young Nikolaos at the rear hatch. He was a hardworking Greek with sharp features and a black, bouncy, mop-top head of hair. A greenhorn, trying to prove himself like me, Nikolaos paced the rear of the vessel, ready to partner with Russell, now on the stern deck above us, to set the gear. Russell would pay out the buoy line, anchor, and running line over the rail. First he'd flip the line down through the stern hatch so Nikolaos could bind it to the first skate of gear.

I replaced circle hooks in a cool rhythm and bounced to the drum beats of the music. Next to me, Daniel asked, "Ya know why pirates wore gold earrings, don't ya?" I had no idea, but I responded quickly with a wild story, "Yeah, they pierced their ears as acupuncture, thinking it would improve their eyesight. Ya know, to forego the eye patch!"

"Wrong!" he said, like a gameshow host. "Pirates wore gold earrings so if their body was found floating at sea, the gold could be sold to pay for a decent funeral." It sounded right to me, but everything was up for debate or a bet on a fishing boat. Fishermen are notorious storytellers famous for "It-was-this-big" exaggerations.

The next thing out of Daniel's mouth, was a horrific scream in slow motion, "NIK·O·LAOS! Y-O-U-R F-O-O-O-T!" The line coiled around Nikolaos's foot like the stranglehold of a python. In seconds, Dean and ponytailed Tito tackled him to the floor; one grabbed his leg and the other slipped and unwound the line, trying not to get caught himself. At the same moment, Larone, who was swift at retrieving fallen fish with a bullhook, slammed the panic button. The vessel instantly backed down, sending a rush of water into the open rear hatch. All deck knives were drawn, ready to cut the line, but it would've already been too late. In every fisherman's head is the warning: "Never stand in the bite of the line." They had just saved Nikolaos's life.

All of us stood silent in shock, except Ed, who had been loading up the autobaiter with partially thawed squid. He shook his Frankenstein head and calmly said, "That was close. Hate to lose him. He's good people." Nikolaos crouched to the wet floor, the color gone from his tan face and his dark eyes tearing up. His curly hair hung, lifeless, soaked with sweat and saltwater. A second of hesitation from Larone and Nikolaos would've launched out the back hatch with the anchor and buoy, like a chunk of bait on a hook, like one of the unlucky seabirds submerged to their death.

Elation, on the other side of terror and fear. He survived. He got a second chance.

Out here we lived each day on the edge between the Heaven and Hell of nature. Did the guys thrive on the risk and the larger-than-life feeling after surviving near death? Would this incident convince any of them to quit fishing while they're still alive? How many near misses would we have on this boat? My mom had gotten a second chance at life, and so did I. How many chances does one get?

Within a month of my go-kart accident, lightning struck again. I walked home from school to find my uncle standing in our apartment doorway. His eyes were red and gut-wrenching intuition blasted a hole through me. My heart already shattered before I could ask him, "What's wrong?" I began to weep before I heard his answer.

"Laura, your father had a bad accident." He hugged me tight; both arms encased me. "I'm sorry Laura. Your dad didn't make it. He died this afternoon."

"N*ooo*, not my daddy!" I screamed into his chest with all the air left inside me. "N*ooo*!"

"I'm sorry, Baby," he said. "I'm so sorry."

Dad had been living in St. Louis. Tom and I missed him so much. I didn't ask my uncle, "How?" All I could ask both him and God was "Why?"

Why?

Why?

Why was life so hard for us? For my brother? For Mom who was willing to take her own life? Why did I almost die a month earlier? Why was I spared while my handsome, thirty-five-year-old dad was gone from this world, and our lives, forever?

My dad was doing the same job he did every day—painting. While his workmate fetched lunch, he worked alone. As he leaned over a parapet on a roof to paint the outside wall of a new addition, he couldn't have known his aluminum paint roller extension would hit an overly slack 7,200-volt power line. Coincidentally, the live wire's protective covers were removed only weeks prior. Did Dad have time for one last prayer to God? Could God or any man have saved him, or was his life over before he even realized the electricity hit him? Two strangers found him lying on the ground with his eyes rolled back in his head and burn marks on his hands. Burn marks were also found on the rooftop.

I wasn't ready to die on this trip, or see someone else die, and I'm sure my father hadn't been ready either when he drove to work that October day. I didn't have a chance to say goodbye to him. Months before my accident, I'd written him a letter. I told him about the fun we had wakeboarding at a lake and apologized for not getting him a birthday present. I ended with "Sorry so Sloppy" and "I Love You." On the back of the envelope there were two horse heads, a foal and a daddy horse, necks entwined. I addressed it, but never sealed or stamped it; I never mailed it. And in my kiddie purse was a plastic card the size of a credit card from Dad that read, "To the Queen of my heart. Carry this card and know that my love is with you wherever you go." I still have both the letter and the card.

At Dad's funeral, he laid in the padded, satin-lined casket. White gloves hid his charred hands; hands that had been burned like those kids in the hospital. I kissed his forehead; it was hard and cold like clay. His spirit lifted out of his body, as mine had after my accident, but his got away, while mine stayed. There lied a wax replica, a mannequin, not my handsome Daddy. I would no longer stand barefoot on his paint-speckled work boots while we slow danced. He would no longer sing Charlie Rich's words, "Hey, if you happen to see the most beautiful girl in the world," to me. I would never again be able to say, "I love you" or "I miss you" to him. I'd never again hear him call me Angel. And so I wondered, as the back end of the flooded vessel drained, could these weeks at sea hold my final breaths and last days without the chance for final words?

In the long term, I learned from wounds, loss and sorrow. My brother lost partial function of his brain as a newborn, and me, a portion of my scalp as a child; both of us lost a father for a lifetime. Though tragic, these experiences shaped my perception and instilled in me a fuller appreciation of the gift of life and the consciousness of its frailty. I was aware of danger, but lived life fully, knowing I might not have tomorrow to try that thing, or make amends, or say "I love you." Today, now, was all we could count on as certain. And now, faced with life-threatening weather and danger all around me, all I could think of was how my poor father died prematurely trying to earn a living, just like I was trying to do in Alaska.

12

～～～

BLACK COD, ORCAS, AND HORSES

WEEKS later, in mid-May, still on our extensive first trip, we moved from the Bering Sea through Unimak Pass to the Gulf of Alaska in search of black cod, which migrate between the continental slopes of the two regions. Black cod, also called sablefish, were sexy fish if you could call them that—dark, sleek, and muscular. Sexy at least compared to P-cod. Each fish, averaging ten pounds and two-plus feet long could live for more than fifty years. We might also see rockfish, because their habitats overlap with our target species of black cod and turbot, also called Greenland halibut, but we were fishing too deep to see many Pacific cod.

Black cod came up on the line from over 300 fathoms, and up to three times deeper, like shiny steel submarines. Their tissues and belly cavity are oily, as with other deep-water pelagic fishes, such as salmon, tuna, and mackerel, or smaller forage fishes like anchovies and sardines. Whitefish, like cod and halibut, which live near the bottom, only have oil in their liver. The oily flesh of the black cod brought a high price and a fat paycheck for the crew when we were "on" the fish. However, they were less abundant than P-cod and harder to find, and I wondered how long it would take to fill our freezer hold at this sablefish pace with a slower catch rate. Though I welcomed the variety of a new fishery and a new region of the Pacific Ocean, I needed a break. Off the boat.

Constant factory noise cranked behind me while I sampled in the factory. I peeked out the gaffing station hatch and yearned for what existed beyond the horizon, just like I had as a teenager on the shores of Lake Michigan. To my delight, pods of orca whales, led by the oldest females, breached and spy-hopped alongside the vessel while squadrons of gulls floated above. The orcas' white oval eye patches, chins. and flanks flashed through the gleaming dark water. They formed social bonds and liked to travel in groups. They had highly stable families and tended not to separate from the oldest female. Witnessing the orcas' graceful power against the high seas, it was hard to believe they could survive captivity like tiny aquarium fishes. At this point, I wished to mount their milky gray saddles and hitch a ride back to port. As awe-inspiring as seeing a snowflake up close or the colors in a rainbow. Was I the only person in the world experiencing such beauty by nature?

As regal as the orcas were, the fishermen grumbled, for they knew our catch would be impacted. Orcas are known to eat birds, marine mammals of any size, and a variety of fish, a particular favorite being the prized black cod.

In the wheelhouse before sampling, I asked Gabe, "How's the catch?"

"Nothing but heads and seaweed," he said, disappointed, shaking his head sideways. Invested in the fisheries and the success of this vessel and crew, I shared his frustration.

Routinely in these waters we pulled miles of line to find sections of it stripped of black cod and turbot. Only their dangling heads were left behind, each one coming up like a middle finger pointed at the fishermen as they approached the rollers. Each orca could eat up to 550 pounds of fish per day. For such enormous mammals, orcas were precise and selective as they dived down near one hundred feet to scout the inbound line for their choice of fish, like an all-you-can-eat buffet of fresh sashimi. They preselected turbot over the nearly identical arrowtooth flounder without tasting them first. Arrowtooth had no economic value because of an enzyme in their flesh that turned it to mush when it was heated. Only a slight difference to the human eye, turbot can be distinguished from the arrowtooth by the shape of their preoperculum, or gill plate, (right angled on the turbot and rounded on the arrowtooth) and the color of their undersides (dusky below the turbot and white beneath the arrowtooth). Amazed at how a 20,000-pound mammal could detect the difference, I wished I could pick out a good man as easily as orcas could pick out a turbot from a lineup of flounders.

The guys were tired of the orcas; I was tired of the guys. I never thought I'd reach the point of super-saturation with these men, with any men. The more the orcas ate off the line, the longer we'd be in search of more fish, and the longer we'd be at sea, wiping our heinies with our seemingly endless supply of toilet paper.

The orcas, rising and falling on the sea, reminded me of carousel horses. I had a strong affinity for both whales and horses. After my go-kart accident and Dad's death, a doctor told my mom, "There's nothing better to get her through trauma and rebuild her esteem than to put her on a horse. It'll give her back some control in her life."

Walter's daughter Margaret rode American Saddlebreds, so I began English equitation lessons, where the rider is judged on their performance, form, and control of the horse. The instructions were clear: "Sit up straight. Shoulders back. Proud chest. Hold your head high. Chin up and in. Tuck your seat. Sink deep into the stirrups.

Grip with your knees. Give clear signals with steady hands." Horses couldn't replace my father, but they filled me with physical and emotional therapy. Horses became my world.

It was 1980 when my own horse Lucy and my new boyfriend Luke trotted into my life. Serendipitous, they even shared the same birthdate, a week before mine. We were all twelve. She was an American Saddlebred with a white blaze down her chestnut face. She, like Luke, was perfect in my eyes. I sketched my school folders full of peanut-shaped, cartoon horse heads; "Laura + Luke" with overlapping letters "TLF" (true love forever); and hearts punctured by Cupid's arrows. The jealous boys called Luke "Richie Rich," because I mistakenly bragged about his thoughtful gifts. Sometimes Luke watched me looping the stable ring during my lessons. Similarly, I'd watch his preteen body lap the pool at his swim meets. I was no longer the sad, pitiful girl with the bald head whose father had recently died. Now I was the girl going steady with the handsome half-Bolivian boy. I was the adventurous one who rode horses. Other city kids rode bikes or skateboards, not horses.

Margaret and I shared a love for horses and cute boys, but we viewed life differently. She was in competition with me and liked boys my age, like Luke, while I just looked up to her as an older sister. She was supposed to look out for my brother and me, but she usually led us on the path to trouble. "Lighten up and join the crowd," she'd say. She hauled us to parties, midnight showings of R-rated movies, or backyard forts full of teenagers sitting in a circle and passing pipes and bongs around.

One night, Margaret, Luke, and I were listening to the Bee Gees in her basement. The lights were dim, except for the disco strobe light and swirling grape globules of the lava lamp. Luke was lying on the floor. She pinned down his arms and said to me, "Kiss him."

"No way. Not in front of you," I said, embarrassed.

"Like this," she added, planting one on the lips of *my* boyfriend. "Go ahead. You'll like it someday."

"Turn around and maybe I will."

I bent down and quickly kissed him, wondering if he could taste my strawberry Bonne Bell Lip Smacker gloss. It wasn't how I had pictured a first kiss, but I guess I liked it. I didn't really know until much later, when we were alone and I could fully absorb the experience. Then he held my hands, pulled me close, and nibbled on my lower lip, taking my breath away.

She tried to get my brother and me to play the asphyxiation game with her friends. The player hyperventilates, and then another person presses them against the wall by their neck to cut off oxygen to the brain. The person goes into an altered state and might get on all fours and bark like a dog, or pass out. Or just die. Tom and I refused to be swayed by the stupid game.

She tried to push us into other dirty deeds—strip poker, smoking, and drinking—to be cool like her. Then Margaret began cutting her boyfriend's name into her arms and picking off the scabs, hoping to scar it into her arm for a lifetime, a homemade tattoo. A beautiful horse, a new red Camaro, expensive shrimp dinners, and all her expenses on Walter's credit card weren't enough to keep her from trouble. I needed to think independently, to avoid following the crowd, especially her lead. I stayed on the straight and narrow, while keeping my little bro tight to my side, far from her influence.

Mom often said, "Pig-face Margaret is a spoiled brat that hasn't worked for anything her whole life."

Margaret would remind me, "Your mom's an abusive bitch."

At times, I agreed with them both. Mom wanted Margaret to have a work ethic, to show more respect and appreciation; Margaret wanted Mom to loosen the reins and not tell her what to do. Neither of them followed rules very well. Both could've used some discipline.

Even if she didn't abide by them herself, Mom had rules for us: Don't drink, smoke, swear, or sass back. Mostly, she diverted us from bad choices. Back in fifth grade I had confessed, "Mom, I want to join a gang."

"Really? A gang? I have a better idea," she said. "Why don't you start a club with your friends instead? You can hold weekly meetings in the basement laundry room. It'll be your own private space."

My *gang* included me and three girlfriends. Our *gang* name: The Bonkers Club. My best friend and I pricked our fingers and rubbed them together to become blood sisters. Then my mom enrolled me in after school dance intramurals, where I learned "The Hustle," and she signed up Tom and me for tae kwon do at the YMCA. Like the orcas, I was social and wanted to belong to something.

My body sprouted from a compact, chunky stump into a lean willow. Towering over my first horse, I moved up to Wild Magic, a dark chestnut with the North Star on his forehead. I competed in English equitation for years, bringing home lots of ribbons and trophies, but rarely did I win final championships. By the time I was fifteen, it was clear that this was a political sport and a rich man's hobby. My competitors stayed in plush hotels and resorts, while my family usually stayed in a twenty-foot camper. I gave in to hormones and the peer pressure of spin-the-bottle with cute boys under the hotel stairwells, ding-dong-ditch in the hallways, and a few water balloons tossed off balconies at passersby. The families of my peers owned things like the Chicago Blackhawks and stables full of horses with famous bloodlines. We bought my horse Magic at a discount auction; Mom said we saved him from the glue factory. But the time came when we could no longer afford a horse on a hairstylist's salary and social security payments—the only gain from my father's death.

Mom seemed more stressed and high strung after Dad had passed away, or maybe I was getting old enough to realize something wasn't quite right. A capable, beautiful powerhouse of a woman, she'd always been my idol, but now it seemed she'd go from hilarious to scary in minutes. Fun, zany Mom spent an afternoon calling all the Chicagoland pet shops listed in the yellow pages to see if we could acquire a chimpanzee as a pet. Frightening, angry Mom raged, threw plates or cups or whatever she had in hand, and would empty the entire silverware drawer in the middle of the kitchen floor if a utensil was put away in the wrong place. There the mess would stay, shiny and scattered, until Tom and I cleaned it up. Behind her back we started to call her Sybil, after the woman in the movie with split personality disorder.

Once, while traveling back home from a horse show in the motor home we stopped at McDonald's. This was when rival Burger King had released their new catchy jingle: "Hold the pickles, hold the lettuce, special orders don't upset us." We ordered inside Mickey D's, then all of a sudden Mom slammed her hand down on the counter. "Let's go!" she said, her hands on our backs urging us to move faster. We followed her out, but wanted to hide, or at least run in the opposite direction. As she stomped out the glass door without our food order, she mumbled, "I'll teach them to put pickles on my Filet-O-Fish the next time I ask!" She fumbled with something outside at the rear of the camper. "Get in!" she ordered. She jumped into the driver's seat, slammed the door, and said, "Buckle up, kids!" She put the pedal to the metal and gunned it.

From the front seat of the camper, I asked, "Mom, what'd you do out there?"

She scooched to the edge of her seat, smiled a mischievous grin, and said, "I pulled the shit shoot! That's what!" She drove a final victory lap around the McDonald's parking lot until we felt a bump. She tore off a small corner of the building's metal roof near the drive thru. A stream of toilet paper and bubbly sewage trailed us out of the parking lot. She cheered in a surge of adrenaline, "That'll teach 'em!" Next stop, Burger King. Where they better not deny her pickles on her sandwich.

That was Mom. Retaliatory at times. Always reactionary. We were unsure whether to laugh, be embarrassed, or be proud of her for standing up for herself, her kids, and any perceived injustices. Most of the time it was an uncomfortable combination of all three.

That was the last big memory of the camper. Money was tight, and the camper would soon be sold, along with some other things.

When I discovered that my horse trainer had been floating our boarding, vet, and farrier bills with deep discounts she could no longer carry, I worked at the barn, a dog kennel, and babysat. Too young to get a legal paycheck, I would do anything to help take the financial load off Mom. I didn't ask for much money outside of the allowance I earned through chores and odd jobs. I wanted to keep my horse hobby, a dream that I knew would eventually have to end. I'd need a car to get to and from school, jobs, and basketball practice. Gas, insurance, new albums. It added up, and I'd have to pay for it. Sadly, my horse, Magic, had to go. But the doctors were right—horses helped me build confidence.

Now, as the groundline came up empty except for black cod heads, I caught my last glimpses of the orcas as they surfaced one more time, before diving down into the ocean and out of sight. That confidence carried me through my up-and-down, merry-go-round life.

13

~~~

BIRTHDAY WISHES

IT was my twenty-fifth birthday, and I'd been wishing upon stars and blue baskets of black cod all week. I hoped to make it back to shore to hear a few familiar voices over the phone; maybe receive a care package in the mail; and buy myself a birthday present, perhaps a new cassette tape since my Sade's *Lovers Rock* was warped from replay. The day arrived, but missing from it were streamers, balloons, having "Happy Birthday" sung to me, and, thankfully, the spanking machine, although several crewmen offered. Instead, Jazz surprised me with a homemade cinnamon roll. It wasn't the triple layer white cake with fresh strawberries and buttercream frosting Mom had spoiled me with in my younger years, but I was grateful. I blew out the one glowing candle wishing for a return to town. As the trail of smoke swirled and disappeared, I knew wishes didn't always come true, and someone's presence wasn't always a gift.

The previous year I was getting reacquainted with Margaret. We hadn't had much contact since she moved to California with her mom. The summer before my senior year in high school Walter retired from print sales in Chicago, and my mom quit her hairstylist job. We packed up, minus Margaret, and convoyed to our new house, this time to the Ozarks of southern Missouri. I was slapped with a large dose of culture shock when on day one we pulled into the only place open to eat, The Hillbilly Bowl. I could only shake my head in disbelief. My favorite Chicago-style Italian beef sandwiches and stuffed pizza were not on the menu. Instead I found chicken-fried steak and biscuits-n-gravy. As we walked in, the hostess greeted us with, "Howdy, ya'll. I'm fixin' to get you seated." We had entered the land of square dancing and country twang. It would be hard to find the R&B music and '80s break dance mixes I favored on the radio.

Despite my resistance to move there, some good things happened, too. We traded up our humble Illinois backyard wetland for a lake view backed by dry, rolling cedar glades. My biggest worry, being a new senior to a new school, was relieved when I was picked to be a starting forward on the basketball team. I would get through this year after all.

The most awesome change came after we moved. Though for years Margaret had called her dad "Walter," like an estranged and distant uncle, Tom and I could officially call him "Dad" now that he had married Mom. The title of stepdad never seemed enough. There was no step between us. The only step he took was into our lives as the fatherhood role was passed like a baton when my biological dad had passed away. Walter was the one who taught me how to ride a bike, fish, change my oil, and sit across from him quietly and read, and be happy just because we were together. He was the dad I needed, and maybe I was the daughter he needed as his own slowly turned him away. Finally, having been uprooted and transplanted too many times, our lives seemed somewhat stable. But maybe it was the reverse for Margaret.

Margaret and I had rarely spoken while I was attending college. Mostly she phoned to ask me how much I weighed, whether I had a boyfriend, and to report Hollywood gossip.

About a month before I moved to Seattle, weeks before my twenty-fourth birthday, I flew to California in an attempt to keep our thin thread of sisterhood from breaking. When I arrived, her car was in the shop, she'd lost her job as a substitute high school teacher, and was near destitute. She blamed a lawsuit, something about a male student pressing charges against her for "inappropriate conduct towards a minor."

Still, we enjoyed a few days together, catching up and reminiscing about the mischief, the fun, and the hard times we'd been through. When the topic of boys came up, so did Luke's name. He'd crossed my mind often mind since he'd moved away, but I had no idea where he was living now. We decided to track him down. We dialed 411 for information. The operator asked for his name, and came up with a match in Florida. Margaret had encouraged our first kiss, and now, more than ten years later, she was the impetus for a long-distance reunion.

Before I left for the airport for Missouri, Margaret said, "I need a big favor. I need you to rent me a car on your credit card for a few days so I can look for jobs. I have no money and can't get my car out of the shop until I get some."

"OK. I guess I can do that." I could help her out. That's what family did. What would a few more days of a rental car matter?

A month later, as I was prepping for my move to Seattle, I received a letter from Margaret—the first time I had heard from her since my visit. It said: "This is some crummy birthday and graduation gift to you. I had to keep the stupid rental car. I do not have the money to pay the tab." What? She had promised to return it after a *few days* and instead kept the car for almost a month? In addition, she told me she had racked up over six hundred dollars in charges on my credit card? Who does that? Certainly not sisters.

Happy Birthday to me? Happy graduation? Happy high-risk fresh start to me.

I left her phone messages, but she never called me back. Instead, I received another letter.

"I am hardly concerned with you having to default on a credit card. . . . If you consider yourself a Christian, I suggest you open up your bible and read it again. . . .We don't have a friendship—we just know each other as some sort of stepsisters because of Walter and your mom."

Whoa! Hold your horses.

Could she really have meant so much more to me than I did to her? I thought we were family, a cohesive orca pod. Now I realized that we saw our combined family in two very different ways. The ending was abrupt. Like a rogue wave, I never saw it coming. But I learned: sometimes you love and give wholeheartedly, then you cut your losses and break away. I forgave her as a Christian, and then tried to forget her as a sister.

Now, a year later, I knew I'd have a fat check, that I'd earned, waiting for me when I got home at the end of my contract. It more than compensated for Margaret's "gift" in the year prior, a bombshell wrapped in a not-so-pretty package. Money. Provision. Independence. I wouldn't end up like Margaret. I would prove that I could take care of myself. On my own. It was my reason for being on this boat. The sea, though filled with daily challenges, was my therapy to help me deal with an erratic past and launch a much needed, brave new start. Aside from Jazz's birthday cinnamon roll, I received two other surprises—my first gray hair and the gift of someone's presence.

Later that night, I quietly made my way to the bathroom to take a shower, traversing through the engineers' room trying not to wake the one who was in there sleeping. Like a mole emerging from a dark tunnel, suddenly popping into the light, I flicked on the switch. Glimpsing in the mirror, I realized I looked more like the guys I was working alongside—like I had been dug out from the bottom of a dumpster—yet it all seemed so normal. My shirt was forever stained in shades of brown and gray, with an occasional orange splotch from contact with a rusty pipe or a wall needing a paint touchup. My layers were infused with fish squeezings, no matter how often Jazz laundered them.

The mirror became less of a focal point for me. I didn't have to primp, inspect my clothes to see if my colors or patterns clashed, check my eye makeup for smudges, or see if my hair was wonky. I traced the outline of my thin neck in the steam building on the mirror. My broad shoulders and arms were becoming stronger each day from hurling baskets full of fish. I gave little thought to how I looked and realized my degree of attractiveness had no value on a fishing boat. My worth was in my job. In being strong. From here forward, I would frown less at my reflection and not look for faults.

I viewed my evening showers as a trip to the spa, providing a tranquil place to rinse away the scales, guts, and goobers from a day of rolling in fish. It was the only time, outside of my rack, when I had privacy. In the shower stall, I laughed and sighed, barely able to stand against the rolls of the ship. Holding onto the slick wall for balance, I scraped free the tiny transparent fish scales that adhered to my face and skin like suction cups, pinching me as they popped loose. My bones thawed as the hot water passed over my cold curves and shot beyond the swaying curtain to the speckled linoleum floor. My towel hung from a hook at a slant, the bottom waving feet from the wall, always in constant motion. I leaned to and fro, my sea legs always bent, ready to buffer the impact of any sudden slams. A razor was a dangerous tool on a moving boat, so shaving my legs would have to wait for stable ground in port.

After my shower, I put on my clean off-duty outfit, basically the same as my on-duty clothes, but this set wasn't allowed in the fish-contaminated factory. Not wanting to disturb the sleeping engineer with the noise from my blow-dryer, even though I'm pretty sure he'd already gone deaf from working in the engine room, I adjusted it to low.

I heard a small tap on the door and thought I woke him up and he's gotta use the head, which means my spa time would be cut short.

I switched off the blow-dryer and said, "Done in a minute," thinking he might go use the other common bathroom.

There was another light knock on the door. He must really have to go. Annoyed, I cracked open the door, "I'm almost . . ." Before I could finish the sentence long, dark fingers followed by a curly head popped through the opening. Russell.

Afraid to wake the engineer, I didn't know whether to tell him to get in or get lost. Which would draw the least attention? I grabbed his thick wrist, jerked him into the steamy bathroom, and closed the door behind us.

"Russell, what the heck are you doing here?"

"I thought I'd wish you a Happy Birthday, and we could talk in private," he said barely above a whisper. "I've liked you ever since I laid eyes on you. You're a beautiful woman, ya know?" He drew closer, and I could see the sweat on his forehead. I'd often craved to have him standing before me without an audience, and now here he was.

I felt like I was in a scene from a movie and the entire audience was on the other side with their ears up to the door.

My pheromones mixed with his cologne, percolating the mist. Every ounce of me wanted this. Backed up against the wall, he put one hand just above my head. I gripped the towel rack to brace and refrain myself. I wanted to jump in, but the larger part of me knew better, yet I said nothing. He dipped his head down, so he was just inches from my neck, and said, "I would really like to . . ."

Rip! The towel rack wrenched off the wall and crashed to the floor with a bang. That's it. Director says, "Cut!" The love scene is over. The engineer had to be fully awake now.

Unsure what to do, I shoved him away with both hands. "Quick! Get out!" I snatched the rack up from the floor. As he tried to reattach the bent screws, I said, "Just leave it. Go!"

When Russell shut the door, I noticed that the engineer's light was on and the curtain to his bunk was open. He was up. And out.

I stood against the closed door trying to regain some composure. I knew the engineer would translate what was nothing into something, and the story would travel through the vessel to the eager audience members. It was inevitable. I would be found guilty. Now I was really ready to get off the ship.

Fortunately, my birthday wish did come true, even if it arrived almost a week late. It was morning, and I was in the wheelhouse when Captain Gabe told me, "Little Miss Snacky Cakes, we're pulling our last string now and then we're steaming back to port. We should hit dock in about eighteen hours."

After fifty-six days at sea with no land in site, my elation was evident: "Hallelujah! Amen, Captain Cookies. Now I know the origin of the word 'longlining.' The workdays are long, and you're a long way away for a long friggin' time."

"Righteous, Dude," he said.

Then I thrust my head out the window, smiled wide, and sang "Happy Birthday to me . . ." at full volume, but not without first hawking a loogie in honor of our daily tradition. I needed to once more hear him say, "*That's* disgusting!"

As we drew closer to port, I became more energized. It had been nearly two months since I'd talked on a land line, read words in a letter, or heard a news broadcast. I'd seen nothing but fish and weather: ice, snow, sleet and waves. I was finally heading back to Dutch Harbor, the cornerstone of this fishing industry. I hoped Stef was in town, but, ultimately, it didn't matter what awaited me as long as I could walk on land again. I longed for a meager day away from the crew and the stories developing out of the towel rack incident. Soon enough I'd be locked up at sea with them for at least another month. The saddest part of heading back to port was losing Captain Gabe, my playful companion. His time was up at the end of this trip, and he would leave this ship—and my side.

Captain Gabe notified the harbormaster of our arrival, "Sécurité, sécurité, sécurité" and shot out some call words over the radio. Soon the rocky coast of Dutch Harbor would appear through the haze. During our time at sea, Captain Gabe had shared much about its history with me.

In the mid-1700s, Dutch was nothing more than a rustic village inhabited mostly by native Alaskan people, Unangans or Aleuts. Later, the natives were enslaved and relocated to The Pribs to harvest fur seals. Dutch was built on mineral-poor volcanic ash, the soil and climate weren't conducive to agriculture, but other commerce thrived. Industry had transitioned from Russian-dominated fur and seal trading to Unalaskan blue fox farming, to gold rush-supported coal-fueling operations for steamships heading north. It then became a World War II base and was bombed by the Japanese in 1942. In the 1950s, Dutch was a major port for Alaskan king crab and by 1978 it had become the biggest shipping and fishing port. Until 1991, just two years before my contract, much of the Bering Sea was dominated by foreign fleets, mostly Japanese and Russian, but changes in regulations converted the fleet from foreign to domestic.

We closed in on the wind-pounded shoreline. I wanted to mix with the locals, sample the notorious rough-house pub culture and soak up the wildness of the Aleutian Islands around me. I hoped for enough time to step foot into the Elbow Room, which had been named one of the top ten most dangerous bars in America. But what's considered dangerous after living and working on the Bering Sea?

We hit Dutch Harbor midafternoon. Captain Gabe had already been out fishing for two months before I boarded. I wondered what it felt like for him to haul a freezer full of fish back to the dock, to have been responsible for the entire crew—for their safety and their paychecks.

The captain and I, attached like a motorcycle and sidecar, rolled down the gangplank and off the vessel. Endangered Steller sea lions swam along the vessel, in search of a handout. I stood off-balance on the stillness of land.

He said, "I'll let you in on a little secret. We captains get bored up there in the wheelhouse for all those months at a time, so we enjoy having you observers along. We're nicer to the girls, though, so we'll get glowing evaluations back in Seattle, and they'll send us more girls. They're more fun to tease, especially when they don't know we're teasing them." He took a deep breath and smiled from dimple to dimple. "Laura, what I'm trying to say is, I especially enjoyed your company."

"Thanks, Gabe. We had a lot of fun, didn't we?"

"Here, I want you to have this." He pulled a winter weight black jacket with a standup collar from his duffel bag. The ship and its name were embroidered on the back. All the fishermen proudly wore them like letterman jackets. "Happy late birthday, Little Miss Snacky Cakes."

I was honored by his gift, and couldn't wait to wear it. "Thanks Gabe. It's awesome. I, I absolutely love it. I can't believe you're giving it to me."

"You put up with a lot of our bullshit. You can hang tough with these guys. If observing doesn't work out for you, you've earned a spot on this vessel." His blue eyes showered me with appreciation. "You will be missed." I was officially part of the fishing gang now.

As he handed me a folded piece of paper, he said, "Here's my phone number in case you're in San Francisco and want a long tour by a good looking short guy with a fabulous personality."

I responded in Gabe's lingo, "Righteous, Dude! I'd like that."

Though Captain Gabe had disappointed me during that one exchange with Captain Hot-n-Bothered, I'd shrugged it off. I hugged him goodbye with immense sadness and wondered how different life would be aboard without him.

"Don't forget to mail this," he said as he handed me the much anticipated letter he'd written to my mom after the incident. "This should comfort your mother for the remainder of your contract," his overgrown mustache hiding the warm smile between his dimples. I would miss that smile. I would miss him.

Although fictional, the letter exemplified his humor and spirit, and perhaps revealed some underlying truths about me.

Dear Laura's Mom,

Although we have never met, I am writing to you as a friend in the desperate hope that you can help us with an irresistible problem that threatens to overwhelm us all. The problem is your daughter. Laura moved aboard the F/V Nomad on April 1. Within two days she had completely cowed and buffaloed my crew. Even Roco Tatum, who is presently on parole from Iron Mountain State Mental Hospital, where he spent most of the 1980s, is completely off his feed and has begun bathing again.

Fishing in the Arctic regions is a brutal and demanding trade requiring rough manly men with large waterproof boots. Yet your daughter, and my nemesis, Laura, now expects the men to join hands in prayer before every meal. Actually, I don't mind the prayers so much, but the hymns have got to go, especially since Leroy insists on singing all the high parts.

While perhaps the language was a bit blue previously, I believe Laura has reversed the pendulum too far. Just yesterday I heard Raoul exclaim, 'Confound it man, I've hooked myself!' These are not the words of a true Alaskan fisherman.

I have serious reservations as to the likelihood of running this vessel with scrubbed, well spoken, polite, calm, respectful fishermen. I tell you, Laura's Mom, it can't be done!

I have only a few questions: Does she always get her way? Can she be stopped? Has she always been like this? Does she ever wear dresses? Do you think she would have dinner with me in Seattle at a decent restaurant if I asked her really nicely? I am perplexed.

Respectfully,
Captain Gabe, Master F/V Nomad

Though written to entertain, his letter deeply touched me. I would miss our traditions, the laughter, and especially our friendship. In that moment, I learned the saddest part of building a relationship at sea is to watch it walk away down the dock toward the airport, likely never to be seen again. Would the crew become the untamable classroom under a substitute teacher? Undeterred, I was almost two-thirds through my contract and would return to the vessel to do my job with renewed energy. I'd celebrated another birthday and had earned one gray hair. I was older and at least a little Bering Sea wiser.

14

∞

TURN AND BURN

WITH the letter in pocket, I anxiously headed for the observer bunkhouse. My options were to walk the muddy, gravel roads; pay an Aleutian Taxi five bucks for one way to anywhere; or, as was common, hitchhike like the locals. After living on a 141-foot ship, any distance beyond its length was considered a long way. I felt like a horse allowed to run free in a pasture for the first time. Land never felt more solid and noticeably stable beneath my feet. I happily shouldered my backpack full of stamped letters and hoofed it. I walked for a mile with pep in my step—and a few jumps, kicks, and skips—before I thumbed a ride. Was it safe? Of course; it's what people did in small island communities. I firmly believe more people are out to help you than hurt you. How could Dutch be any different? The first truck stopped, and I hopped in the back among a tethered crab pot and line. I had a plan of escape—drop, cover, and roll out of the truck bed—if I needed to. But for now I enjoyed the ride. No haulbacks. No motion of the ocean. Just the sound of kicked up gravel on glorious, bumpy ground. Apart from the driver and the bald eagles, more plentiful than seagulls, flying overhead, I was alone.

The plan was for a turn and burn: hit the dock for twelve or so hours, just enough time to offload our product; backload groceries, supplies, and fuel; and head back to sea. All I could do now was hope for bad weather offshore, so threatening that it might keep us tied to the dock an extra day. Curfew was firmly set at midnight, even though we'd probably leave later. Captains kept the guys working so town time—read: free time for crewmen to get into trouble— was kept to a minimum and the real departure time under wraps. Deprived crewmen, ravenous for all they'd been denied, couldn't be expected to behave responsibly. It wasn't unusual for them to go AWOL from the boat while in port, possibly ending up smashed on the beach after a drunken night of partying, in jail, or just left behind. Though the boat's schedule wouldn't allow me to spend the night at the bunkhouse, tour the island, or step into the Elbow Room, I had time for my foremost goals before curfew: food, phone, and mail. The offshore forecast looked decent, so there was nothing to prevent us from leaving on time, before sunrise.

I gleefully hopped out of the back of the truck and thanked the fisherman for the lift. As I opened the door to the bunkhouse, my first words to the observer coordinator were, "Is Stephanie in town?" Sadly, she'd left on her vessel days before. A small bit of joy drained out of me. I had hoped to see my new best friend and share stories.

Compared to the *Nomad*, the observer apartment was plush with homey furnishings: unbolted, freestanding couches, chairs, and lamps; tables not covered in green grippy net; cushioned area rugs that I could walk on in my socks; and wall decorations. A gray tabby meowed and serpentined around my legs. I knew what it felt like to crave that contact, to want a hand to reach out to comfort you. I was never so happy to see a cat in all my life. I knelt down to stroke her soft fur. Who needed whom more?

I had popped out of a time warp; the television reported baseball and hockey highlights, weather, and what I cared to miss—the blow-by-blow news coverage of tragedies from around the world that had happened while we were at sea.

Another observer invited me along to dinner at the airport restaurant. We could walk? Yes, please! Like a desperate hound kenneled for almost two months, I couldn't say yes fast enough. When I'd first stepped off the plane in Dutch, the small airport seemed desolate, like a closed movie set from an old spaghetti Western, but now I saw it as the most civilized place on the island. I downed a hearty cheeseburger, JoJos, and a fresh green salad—the supply of fresh veggies had been depleted aboard ship after a few weeks. I dropped my letters, including the special one to Mom from Captain Gabe, into a mailbox. It seemed more like years than two months of being out of touch with the mainland.

The airport breezeway was one of the few indoor places where you could make phone calls out of the elements. The other observer went back to the bunkhouse while I stayed behind to exchange months of missed highlights with family and friends.

First, I phoned Luke with a calling card; there was no answer, so I left a message on his answering machine.

Next, I called Mom. "Hello? Ma'am, this is the operator. Will you accept a collect call?" Thrilled that she answered, I jumped up and down as far as the snake-like metal cord allowed.

She shrieked, "Laura? Is that you?"

"Yes! I'm finally off the boat." I could hear her holding back the tears.

"You're back in Seattle?"

"No, I'm in port," I said. "I'm at a payphone in Dutch Harbor." It sounded good to my own ears, too.

"Oh, I was so worried about you. I'm glad you're okay." I pictured her clenching her hands to her chest, balling up her flannel nightgown.

Through her sobs, I shared stories of my lengthy trip on the high seas. I also forewarned her about the letter she'd soon receive from Captain Gabe.

I squeezed in a few minutes with Walter. An ex-Navy man, he knew ships. He wanted details—the storms, the amount of ice, where I slept, was I seasick, did the guys drink Aqua Velva like they did when he was in the Navy? And what *did* I do out there anyway? He could relate. He was the one I'd go to when I needed advice. He was interested. He asked about *me*. But in typical form, Mom grabbed the phone away from him before we could finish. I always had to say, "Tell Dad I love him."

"What are you going to do now? Are you going back to Seattle for graduate school?" she asked me, fearing my plans may had changed. She urged me toward land—where I'd continue college, get a real job, meet a man, get married, and have children—where she could easily call me.

"What about all those jobs you applied for in Seattle?" she asked. "Did you hear back from any of them?"

"Not yet, Mom. I've been at sea the whole time. There are no phones or mail out there. I haven't seen a Help Wanted section or a single newspaper in two months. My contract isn't up for at least another thirty days." I thought of all the work I'd done to get this far and the long list of rejections I had left behind in Seattle.

"Well, I don't want to see you working on those fishing boats all your life."

"Me neither, Mom. But now I can buy you a nice gift or take us both on a trip with the money I earn." Though the positives outweighed the bad, I certainly wasn't ready to say I wanted to go back to sea. The cash was a big draw. The pay from a job on land couldn't compare.

"Why don't you move back here to Missouri?" she pleaded. "You could work at the state fish hatchery again. You know the guys there love you."

Mom had been trying to convince me to come back since the day I left. Walter, although sad to see me leave, said, "You will need two raincoats in Seattle, because one will always be wet." Then he helped me map my route out of the Ozarks.

At times I still thought myself foolish to have branched out so far away from family in the Midwest and try to take root in Seattle. As I walked the gravel road back to the bunkhouse, my land worries and life decisions came into focus. What was to come in my future back in Seattle with all of the pressures of trying to make it on my own—graduate school, a career, the guy, and family? What would happen with Luke and I? Maybe I would be pushed back to the Ozarks in desperation if a career didn't work in my favor. Though I would reapply to UW's graduate program in fisheries, my chance of acceptance was slim. Maybe I wasn't smart enough, didn't have the right connections, or wasn't enough of a salmonhead, as the professor from Arkansas had warned. I could waitress again as a last resort, but then I thought, *could I?* Thinking about my unknown future was overwhelming.

Before returning to my vessel, I sped through the community mailbox. I left a few letters for Stef and found a hearty stack of letters addressed to me. I hugged them tight to my chest. People had thought of me while I'd been gone. Bliss. I nestled into an overstuffed couch and delved into all I'd missed.

There was a package from Luke, which I saved for last. Mom's letters were warm and sincere. One said, "I miss being able to talk to you, to call you when I'm slow at work, or bored or need a lift." Another she'd written when Walter and Tom were gone for a week, "I now know what it feels like to be a childless widow." The last one read, "You've been a real blessing to Dad [Walter] and me. You're all a parent could ever dream of having in a daughter." The letters were full of I love yous, I miss yous, and her famous signoff, "Hugs and fishes." Distance makes you realize what you have or had. Mom was lonely, too.

Many of my friends wrote at least one note, but most of the mail was from Stephanie. Her letters unfolded with story after story, beginning with the moment we'd dropped her at her vessel on our first day. In addition to being flooded by potential roommate offers, she was immediately approached by a wild-eyed guy with no teeth and rotting gums. He was out on Huber (temporary work release from prison) and wanted the alcohol we used to preserve fish otoliths (ear bones). With booze unavailable after long periods at sea, they'd drink it, regardless of proof. This is akin to what Walter had said about the Navy guys drinking Aqua Velva aftershave. Stef's crew tried to drink her otolith alcohol. Vodka, Aqua Velva, otolith alcohol. "Same. Same," as the Vietnamese guys might say. Why had my crew not tried this with me yet?

Stef, however, like myself, had been assigned the dissection of twisted cod stomachs that didn't use alcohol as a preservative. Instead, we stored the samples in vials of formalin. My crew tried to eat my samples; Stef's crew brought other antics. She wrote:

> On my first day of sampling, there I was in my corner of the factory, I thought alone, slicing through cod stomachs and squeezing out the mixed lunch. I picked up the next huge cod, and when I slit open its belly, it spewed out a pure load of eyeballs! I was dumbfounded! Where did this single cod find so many eyeballs to eat at one time? Speechless, I was ready to bag 'em up in formalin when I heard snickering, then laughter, from a seasoned processor across the room. He'd rammed his fist down that cod's mouth, ripped the guts out, packed it with a bunch of eyeballs, and then slipped the fish back into my sample basket when I wasn't looking. Can you believe I almost fell for it?

She'd also witnessed a crewman urinating in the factory, but her Peeing Man bragged of his deed too much. The captain found out and formally wrote him up for sexual harassment. Peeing Man blamed Stephanie, even though she blew off the incident like I did and never reported it. I wondered if she had an Underwear Man aboard, too?

Letter after letter, Stef described experiences and fixations much like my own. Her words were exactly what I needed to hear. We were in this adventure together—our friendship forever sealed. She had also spent months drooling over men as they tied knots, mended nets, climbed rigging, and secured gear to the railing. Her letters confessed she had the hots for one of the Latino deck-hands. "Muy picante!" she exclaimed. "Crushes aren't equivalent to fraternizing or 'emotional involvement,' are they?" Wait until she reads about Russell, my obsession with his *Obsession*, his raising the anchor, and our steamy encounter.

"Surely they don't expect us to only observe fish and whether garbage is being tossed overboard?" she continued. "There's more to look at than that, and I'm not talking whales or scenic landscapes."

We thought much the same, and had both sent silly poems to each other. She would read mine the next time she hit port.

Same Old Thing
by Observer Laura

It's only been two months. Seems like all year.
I don't really drink, but I need a beer.
At first it was just another adventure.
A job. Now I'm not quite sure.
Romping, bucking, steaming this ocean.
Now I only wish something would stop this motion.
I once could smell the crisp fresh air and on a star I'd wish.
Wish now I couldn't smell stale cigarettes and fish, fish, fish.
Same old thing, day in and day out.
Oh, what I'd give to freely walk about.

For example, look what this day has brought:
Rockfish, codfish, halibut, and an old crab pot.
And let me guess what tomorrow will bring.
No. I already know. The same old thing.
This work is getting tiresome, boring, and monotonous.
So, why did I come out here knowing this?
Good question. I ask myself that each day.
I guess I'll give it up to God and pray it away.
It's the only thing I can do to get me through this season.
Why am I here? Money is the reason.

Stephanie's retort in her own poetic voice.

Boat Life—I'm So Damn Tired
by Poor Stephanie

I'm tired of simple challenges like opening a door with a hot cup
of coffee or standing on one leg to put on my pants.
I'm tired of Shower Tilt-A-Whirl; naked skin on icky walls and
moldy curtain.
I'm tired of swinging blue baskets, length frequencies, and fat,
ugly, slimy cod.
I'm tired of galleys and heads, green grippy net on tables and
counters, guard rails on my rack.
I'm tired of being told I'm beautiful, tired of the paranoia that
there's a peephole to my room or the shower.
I'm tired of XtraTufs, being rubberized in bright orange and hats
on the rare sunny day for fear of being shit on.
I long for sandals and tank tops, a kitchen, a bathroom, an
obedient latte, a full hot tub, and fish, already dead, from a menu.
I long for stillness and true love.
I'm just so damn tired.

We weren't in town at the same time, but we thrived from one another's humor and positive attitude shared through our letters. It gave us strength—strength we would surely need in our third month at sea.

At last I held the package from Luke. I hadn't seen him since I was in Missouri visiting friends and family a few months before my at-sea adventure. It had been a hard week, with Mom acting out and blowing up daily, if not hourly. I was once again trying to bring my family together, to make it whole, to enjoy some time with them before I shipped out to Alaska, where I might, perhaps, I don't know, die in a big raging storm. There were several more days before I could fly back to Seattle—the pricey airline change fee kept me hostage, with little choice but to wait out her yelling. I called Luke for a listening ear and hopefully gain another perspective.

"Come stay with me for a few days," he said. "I'll fly you to Miami. It's on me."

"But all I have with me are winter clothes. It's over seventy in Florida," I reasoned

"I'll buy you some clothes and shoes. It's only for a few days," he replied, taking away any of my concerns.

"Let me think about it . . . Yes."

The next day, I stood at the baggage claim in the cool Miami airport with boots, jeans, and a bulky black turtleneck sweater, nervous to see my eighth-grade sweetheart after ten years. I turned to see his warm cocoa eyes meet mine. He handed me a giant bouquet of flowers, which took me straight back to junior high and his thoughtful gifts—the framed picture of a puppy cuddling a kitten, the one he'd bought at Hallmark, was hanging on the wall of my Seattle apartment. "The flowers are beautiful, Luke. Thank you. You look the same." Translation: he still rocked my world.

"You're as beautiful as ever, Laura P.," he said, wrapping me in a hug. "*Bienvenido a* Miami. Let's go buy you a nice outfit so we can get rid of that turtleneck. We have dinner reservations tonight."

We spent four enchanting days together, getting to know each other as adults. He overflowed with affection and generosity. One late night after a dinner cruise, we walked hand inhand, barefoot along the beach, searching deep into starry skies and each other. A narrow path led us from the champagne-bubble surf to a giant sea turtle laying her eggs in the sand. I thought of my dad cutting up the six-pack rings so they wouldn't wrap around the head of a bird or a turtle like this one. We watched her strain and struggle, finally releasing her eggs into the hole she'd dug. The turtle blinked salty tears, and I shed a few, too. I was sad for the distance between Luke and me, sad for the loss of my father, and sad to feel disconnected from the family I did have. The baby sea turtles would find their way out to sea; I would eventually find my way, too.

All at once Luke interrupted my thoughts. "Hey, let's drive to the Keys," he suggested.

"Now? I want to sit here and watch this turtle. This is a miracle of nature," I said. "Plus, it's two in the morning and we don't have a change of clothes."

"We'll stop at my apartment, then we'll go. We can still catch the sunrise." And we did.

Luke got what he wanted when it wasn't generally available, or he'd push until there were no more options. In restaurants he'd ask for dishes not listed on the menu because he was in the mood for something else. He'd ask, "Could you please ask the chef if he'd prepare me Snapper Francaise?" Like a genie out of a bottle, they'd grant his wish.

Sporadically during the two-hour drive to the Keys I heard, "I really want to hear some Bob Marley. We have to find a place to buy a cassette. I gotta hear that song."

"Okay, Rain Man," I said, mocking his repetition. Of course, most every place was closed between Miami and the Keys in the wee hours of the morning. We pulled into every Ma and Pa side-of-the-road store or gas station just in case they sold music, Bob Marley's *Buffalo Soldier*, more precisely.

In the Keys, we arrived to our oceanfront suite before breakfast. The warm waters before us couldn't be more different than the Bering Sea. Luke asked, "Can I get you anything, Baby Doll?"

Except for a nap, how could I need anything else? This place, this moment in time, was perfect. I looked at our grand view from the terrace. Knowing he always asked for things outside of what was available, I pointed to a nearby palm tree and said, "Yeah. I want one of those coconuts."

He slid open the screen and looked back at me with his sexy brown eyes, fully aware I had purposely challenged him. He jumped over the railing to the beach, and to my surprise scaled up the curved trunk without hesitation. He ran back in and tossed the coconut on the chair like a hairy football. We hugged and he nibbled my bottom lip, like only he knew how to do. Then asked, "*Que mas, mi amore?*" What more, my love?

He would harness the moon for me if I'd asked him. No goal, no request, nothing was too far out of reach. I loved that about him. Our fire had grown from the sparks of eighth-grade kindling.

Now in Dutch Harbor, the miles between us vanished as I unwrapped the package he had sent. My hands warmed as I caressed the cover of a handcrafted burgundy notebook. Stitched on cloth were gold words in cursive, "Letters from the Heart." Webster's definition of love was typed on the first full page. Page two said, "Without your presence, my words are the strongest expression of my love I can give you. I pray my words inspire you and light new paths for your life . . ."

The next twenty-four pages were handwritten letters, each one in its own plastic sleeve; he wrote one to me each day for three weeks. The letters began: My Lady P, My Love, or Baby Doll. In them he described a growing love for me and encouraged me to move to Florida to be with him. He would support me through graduate school if that's what I still wanted. Support. I could use a double dose of that.

He'd also enclosed Grover Washington's *Winelight* CD and the words to "Just the Two of Us," as sung by Bill Withers: "We can make it if we try. Just the two of us." Could we? Could I love him blindly as my teenage self had? Were a few days spent together, many phone conversations, and a notebook of letters enough to lead us into forever?

Several times I'd begun writing to him to tell him I'd consider moving to Florida to be with him. My love for him felt real, but so did the blazing red flags. Luke could surge from a small craft advisory to a hurricane warning in seconds.

On day three of my short visit with him, we sped down Alligator Alley through the Everglades in his shiny black car, the leather seats warmed as the sun beat down through the sunroof. With each gear shift and press of the pedal his adrenaline amplified, his thirst for risk unquenchable. In that moment I saw he would never be satisfied.

"Okay, this isn't fun anymore," I said, aggravated. "Please slow down."

His smile turned into a devilish sneer. Just as I asked, "Luke, what's the rush?" the car spun out of control. I held on tight and felt the rush, the fear, like on the ship while waiting for the next wave to strike. Then, slam! Gravel, dust, and chunks of grassy earth shot from all around us. When the washing machine finally stopped, he calmly turned toward me with a mischievous grin and said, "Sorry, Laura. You were right. I was going too fast." He drummed the steering wheel and said, "Wooo, man, *this* is why I drive a lease car."

Manic? Probably. Dangerous? For sure. I loved one side of him; I feared this other half more.

It was my last night in Fort Lauderdale when he said, "I need to make a quick stop to check out an investment property." Luke had dropped out of high school, got his GED, and put himself through college. His noble goal was to renovate homes, improve neighborhoods, and provide affordable housing. This was his first offer on a dilapidated house. We crept down a driveway and found the house behind unkempt hedges. There were more than a few broken windows. He reached into the glove box, and I thought he was getting out a flashlight. I was right, it was a flashlight . . . and a gun.

"Are you kidding me?" I asked. "You keep a loaded gun in your car?"

"Yeah, this is a drug den. Gotta be streetwise in this business. I never know when someone might come out swinging a lead pipe at me."

He was determined. A do-er. A fixer. But could I trust him fully? Would I feel safe?

As much as my heart loved Luke and my body was ready to get out of the cold and brutal Alaska weather and be warmed by the sun, the sand, and someone's arms, I wadded up the letters and started again, writing something more sensible. I listened to the persistent whispers. I wasn't moving to Miami yet. Don't rush into this. Give it time.

For the past two months at sea, I'd stepped out of the universe, out of space and time and reality. I had only hours in port to reconnect before I'd have to hit pause again. Real life seemed distant and hazy, like a dream, but all dreams seemed possible on the Bering Sea. A real career? True love? Sure, it was all possible. If I could endure living on a commercial fishing vessel for months at a time, I could overcome other obstacles. Challenges on land seemed small when you were out fishing on the vast and wild seas of Alaska.

With curfew upon me, it was time to lay a patch, turn and burn. I pried my body and mind from the comfort of the bunkhouse—duty called. On the way out, I passed the large bedroom with its roomy bunk beds and thick mattresses I would not rest upon. The gray tabby rubbed against my XtraTufs as I slipped them back on. Her tail twitching as if to say, "I know how you feel."

It was ten o'clock, and I rode back to the vessel under the late Alaskan sunset. Spring's seventeen hours of daylight would help make sea time more bearable, despite the temperatures hovering just above freezing. The daylight hours would lengthen and the temperature would increase until the summer solstice—a day I hoped to enjoy in Seattle. June 22 would mark the one-year anniversary of my move.

I scanned scenic tundra—gray and brown rolling hills still topped with snow and dwarf-shrubs growing prostrate without a tree in sight. World War II remnants tucked away in the hillsides. A half-century earlier, in June 1942, Dutch Harbor was the only North American land bombed by the Japanese, except for Pearl Harbor. As a result, the majority of the native Aleuts were evacuated and transferred to Southeast Alaska.

Some thought the reason for the bombing was to sever the supply line between the United States and the USSR. Another belief is that the Japanese wanted to divert US forces from Midway (a Pacific Island approximately halfway between Alaska and the Hawaiian Islands) to the Aleutians, thereby leaving Midway more vulnerable to a Japanese invasion. Perhaps the government kept the Dutch Harbor and Aleutian attack under wraps, fearing Americans would panic if they knew the close proximity of the Japanese fighters. Ironically, the Japanese are still one of the top foreign trade partners in the Alaskan fishing industry in this area that was once the setting of a war between us. An American ship, the SS *North-western*, now the remnant rusty bow of the vessel, no more than a bird perch, sits above the tide in Captain's Bay with the back end, grounded and sunk into the deep, a reminder of history.

As I headed back to the boat, I wished for more time to steep in Dutch's history; it could be a long while before I set my eyes or feet on this rock again. But I was headed back to my 360-degree view of ocean and sky for another month. I knew I would face new challenges, but I had at least gained confidence in my job. I clutched my letters, small reminders that I wasn't alone, and reboarded my vessel, leaving one world for another.

15

DOWNWARD SPIRAL

WITHIN a week I learned the second trip would be very different from the first. Along with Captain Gabe, we'd changed out some of the crew in port. The wheelhouse warmth and funhouse atmosphere that upheld me through the previous tough months at sea had drifted away. My place of refuge was no more. Now we were under little, if any, direction from less-than-concerned Captain Gus. He had stringy blond hair and a black dot on the white of his eye. He seemed burned out, too early to be due to work exhaustion; I suspected something else in his life. He didn't smile or smirk; his face remained frozen in a scowl. There would be no more "Good morning, Little Miss Snacky Cakes" greetings to start my day. Captain Gus kept the wheelhouse under a gag order, with conversation kept to a minimum and the heavy metal cranked to the max.

The spirit of the boat spiraled downward with each launched anchor and set line. I felt fortunate to have a couple months of experience under my belt. I couldn't imagine what my first trip as a novice would've been like had Captain Gus been running the vessel instead of Captain Gabe.

My wheelhouse joy had been displaced by a killjoy, so I retreated to neutral territory, the galley. I spent more time with Jazz, playing rummy or cribbage, making friendly bets with the few belongings we had aboard: articles of clothing, cassette tapes, and books. I lost my favorite hooded Chicago sweatshirt to him—it was way too small for him anyway and I tried to win it back. We cooked more together now. I would challenge him to prepare whatever delicacies I caught in my samples, like the live octopus I presented to him suctioned to the hood of my rain gear. He'd say, "Man, why you bringing me that? Leave it there on the deck," knowing it would crawl away and he wouldn't have to cook it. I continued to help in my two self-appointed daily assignments: filet fish for each meal and bake dozens upon dozens of homemade chocolate chip cookies.

One morning while paddling through a vat of cookie batter, I wrinkled my face. "Jazz, I smell something nasty. Kinda musty." I sniffed my way through the galley, opening lids and doors. "Don't ya smell it?" I zeroed in on it like a shark to chum. "It's there," I said, pointing to door number three. Whatever *it* was, resided in the cabinet under the sink.

Jazz wiped his meaty hands on a dish towel. "Shhh," he said, putting a finger to this lips. He stood on tiptoe, scanning the doorways for any onlookers.

I opened the cabinet. Next to the Pine Sol and yellow rubber gloves sat a plain white five-gallon bucket. Jazz pried off the lid, still looking around the galley. Inside, the foaming purple liquid looked like the punch in the recirculating dispenser on the galley's opposite wall.

I took a whiff, and it made my head snap back. "Yuck! What is that?"

He paused, waiting for my neurons to fire and my scientific deduction to kick in. "It's grape juice!"

"Grape juice?" I crinkled my nose. "Grape juice and what?"

"Yeast. Ya want some?" he asked, forming question marks with his eyebrows.

"That's what I smelled? Homebrew? No, I wouldn't touch it with a ten-foot pole gaff." Having seen how alcohol could ruin people made it easy to refuse his offer.

He scooped out a cupful, took a sip, and put the lid back on the bucket. He smiled wide. "It's not quite ready."

Would it ever be ready?

It was late morning, and I suspected that the crew had already been sampling the not-so-fine wine way before its time. Having just left town a week earlier, the guys already needed a fix and couldn't wait for full fermentation or for the real stuff when we returned to Dutch.

I never fully believed my stepdad's tales of desperate Navy guys drinking Aqua Velva, but then Stef had told me about her crewmen trying to get at her otolith alcohol. Now my crew was half-crocked, and I wondered if this was the reason for some of the mischief. I guessed this viticulture hobby had been only one of the many secrets kept from me in my insular bubble of innocence. This was the backdrop of everyday life on this fishing boat. No thanks, Jazz. I didn't want any homebrew, but now I was an accomplice to the deed . . . guilt by association.

The homebrew may have partially fueled the succession of events that occurred over the following weeks. I thought maybe the poor catch or lack of encouragement from the captain lowered morale. Whatever the reason—too much saltwater between the ears, love shakeups over the phone while we were in town, or just plain homesickness—the bad attitude spread like a virus through our floating home, attacking Captain Gus, Jazz, and the rest of the crew. Order quickly unraveled.

I went to Russell in search of an answer. "What is the deal around here? Have you told anyone about your breaking and entering into my bathroom?"

Russell stood tall, up close, with his cologne fading beneath his sweat. "No, of course not. I swear," he whispered.

"Then why the suspicious looks from everyone?" I asked, wondering if I was just being paranoid like Jazz watching over his homebrew.

"Maybe it's the engineers. They must have spread rumors."

I didn't think it was possible. The engineers were nice guys, introverted. My throat tightened as I tensed up. The crew knew I was closer to Russell than the others. But whatever stories were divulged, they were pumped full of i-*man*-gination. And I doubted that Russell would deny any gossip to spare my reputation. The talk would make him look good. Whoever won over the girl was declared the winner. I really wanted to trust him, but could I?

To my surprise, the all-male crew was far more gossipy than any pack of teenage girls or group of busybodies. Sudden silence and sneers met me in the galley. Twisted tales of my innocent bathroom escapade with Russell had traveled through the boat like missiles launched to seek and destroy. The made-up stories would be far more entertaining than the truth.

As I tallied the fish and days aboard, agitation compounded around me. Was I to blame for the turn in temperaments, or was I the easiest target on which to unleash their frustrations? They knocked me where I was weak: anchor time. They'd shout, "Yeah, anchor time. Get some!" And now when I wore newly traded clothes it caused an uproar. I'd hear, "Hey, Laura got into So-and-so's pants," or "What'd you have to do get her shirt off of her?"

I acted like their comments didn't bother me, but they were wearing me down and warping me, like one of the overplayed cassettes we'd exchanged. I told myself to roll with it like each over-powering wave.

Underwear Man still lurked on the ship, taking every opportunity to provoke me with his "Mmm, mmm, *mmm*s," and the lick of his lips. I tried to shake it off and ignore him, but he creeped me out. I tried to go to bed before him, so he couldn't watch me from behind as I wiggled into my upper bunk. Though Captain Gabe had banned porn from the common areas, that rule seemed to disappear with Captain Gus in charge. Now Underwear Man purposely left his bunk curtain open so I could see him fondle the wrinkled pages of his girly magazines.

He revved up the others, too. Between bites of pancakes at breakfast, I overheard a portion of my fictional love life spread across the galley tabloids. "Russell said it was good for him last night," he said, drawing in the crowd. "I wonder if it was good for her?"

Her? Was I invisible? I was sitting right here! Being the only "her" on board, I had to consider if this was a moment when I should blow a gasket or blow it off.

"Well, considering I was standing in the room with all my clothes on talking in front of five of you with all your clothes on, I'd have to say my all-night love affair was disappointing," I launched back. "Just like you guys." I grabbed my plate and left the galley. There was nowhere to go and no one to comfort me.

Involved conversations with any one crew member were blown into tales of intimate romance. In this case, gender made a difference. A male observer could stand unnoticed talking within arm's distance to a crewman in a stateroom, the galley, the factory, or a narrow hallway. As a woman, this same discreet chatter, whispers, or laughter was seen as picking favorites, regarded as a hot romance and fuel for fishermen-scripted soap operas. The machine-gun firing of stories exhausted me.

For most of my young adult years I'd stayed on the straight-and-narrow and surrounded myself with supportive friends. I'd never experienced gossip about me before, at least that I was aware of, and didn't quite know how to handle it. All were guilty, and to my disappointment, I suspected those I felt close to: Jazz, Dean, and maybe even Russell. The friendship that I so desired was both my solace and my source of pain. Friend or foe? They changed like the Bering Sea weather.

I needed a respite from the guys, but escape to where? I thought I would find peace away from all the drama when I left Missouri for Seattle, but suddenly it was hard to find in the middle of an Alaskan ocean.

Relative privacy could be found behind the blue drape of my rack, if laying down in a dark room is how I wanted to spend my time. I also had the magic slot, the half hour between shifts when no one was sleeping in my room. I didn't have to tiptoe or be quiet or keep the lights off or be on lookout for Underwear Man. I crouched on the floor between the men's discarded piles of clothes and flip-flops. I would read with my back against the locker or do pushups and sit-ups while listening to songs such as C+C Music Factory's "Gonna Make You Sweat" and Deee-Lite's "Groove Is in The Heart" on my Walkman. I was alone for a few precious minutes.

On good weather days solitude could be found on deck. As the late spring air warmed by a few degrees, that's where I would go. I could write in my journal or jump rope. Then I found my own space hidden away from both the guys and the wind on deck in a watertight storage locker double the size of a standup freezer. After I rearranged the bulky irregularly stacked piles of coiled line, I could sit comfortably with the heavy door open to a view of the sea. It was my secret fort, my reprieve, where I could read, listen to my Walkman, pray, and be alone.

One morning, sleep deprived after a night of being pummeled by weather, I headed to my outside burrow for some *me* time. I opened the ship's starboard door to the calm after the storm: tranquil seas and a fog-filled sky. However, I wasn't alone at all. Looking both forward and aft I saw about forty dark birds, what I thought to be auklets, about the size of a palm, scattered on the deck, like lost tennis balls hit outside the fence. Some of the auklets were hunkered down along the interior wall. Many had tucked themselves behind tethered buoys, next to the crane, and into pockets of space in the gear. Others had flipped over on deck, their little webbed feet in the air, dead from impact.

In gusty weather at sea, phenomena known as "bird storms" occur. Flocks of windswept birds lose their way and get knocked into a vessel's rigging or land en masse. The auklets had escaped to this fishing boat to seek shelter from erratic weather. The ship had been their rescue, a safe haven, a solid island in the storm, but now it threatened their lives. The birds didn't fully know the obstacles they would face until they landed. Unable to capture enough wind from the semi-protected deck, they were now trapped.

I scooped up several of the frightened puffs, light as a whisper, and held them close to my chest and the warmth of my body beneath the padded army jacket I wore. I wished someone would do the same for me.

When I was growing up, Mom would brush my long hair and then tell me to clean out the bristles. She said, "Put the hair in the crook of a tree. Maybe a bird will use it to make a nest." I'd check daily, and when it disappeared I imagined it woven together with twigs and moss, keeping baby birds safe, comfortable, and warm.

Now on deck, as I held two of the little black seabirds it was hard to imagine their journey. How far had they flown from their home when their path had been wildly interrupted? What was the right thing for me to do? Let them figure it out on their own against the whim of Mother Nature? Would they able to hurdle the raised edge of the deck that stood taller than their little bodies? If they hopped to the center of the open bow they could probably take flight. What should I do?

Flocks of gulls floated on the glassy sea around us. I said a quick prayer, "Dear God, please save some of these birds." I took a breath, closed my eyes, and launched handfuls overboard to set them free. I couldn't look, but I hoped to save more than I drowned. A light breeze passed by, filling me with fresh salty air.

Just when I began to relish a bit of happiness, the daily tabloids hit the stands. As I headed up the ladder to the aft deck, green-eyed Dean opened my secret fort, the storage locker, to see the gear evenly arranged instead of in loose piles the way he'd left it. He watched me as I stepped up the last rung.

"Well, well, Darlin', I see we have a little love nest in here," he accused.

Silence. What could I say? Why bother? Would he even understand that I needed some space, a bit of peace away from the guys? Even if it was as absurd as hiding away in a storage locker? There always seemed to be another subtle blow, another wrenching comment waiting for me around every turn. Maybe the next story would put Dean at the center of the developing plot.

I hadn't before looked at my hideaway as a love nest, but maybe I would now. Was it time to indulge them and invite Russell into my lair? With the crew, I stood guilty either way.

This moment reminded me of something I'd heard: if a winter puffin is uninterested in the companionship of his fellows, he becomes a forgotten bird, solitary on the open sea. I stood alone with the puffin. I turned portside, toward the open sea and away from Dean, and scanned the lower deck for more trapped birds.

The men's comments didn't stop with me. They continued to mock Captain Gabe, even though he was long gone, referring to him as Academy Boy. They considered his license a Cracker Jack toy, because he didn't work his way up the ladder from a factory processor, to deckhand, to deck boss, to mate, and finally to captain—the route taken by most other captains fishing in Alaskan waters. In the crew's minds, Gabe was gay, and his deep-voiced girl-friend, Alexia, was actually a man named Alex. The fact that she had a daughter didn't matter; they'd say it was a coverup. Their "proof" was that Captain Gabe was from San Fran-swish-co, California, as they called it. From the conversations I'd shared with Gabe, I knew he *really* liked women, and no matter what they said, I still adored him.

The crew jabbered on about the Japanese technicians as a group, how they were all feminine, flip-flopping around in those pastel rubber sandals too small for their feet. The Japanese delicately waved their wrists around like ballerinas. The crew would demonstrate, placing their hands on relaxed hips with their fingers pointed down "like women." Since all four of the Japanese shared a room, well, that must have mean they shared each other's bunks, too. The crew said Captain Gabe gave the technicians special treatment because he was *one of them*. At some point, I think the crewmen actually believed the stories they concocted, but I didn't believe anyone.

Still, I wasn't completely defeated or deterred. After I finished my own duties, I continued to work alongside the guys in the factory or baked cookies and cooked in the galley with Jazz. His moods went up and down with the barometer, changing under atmospheric pressure and peaking more regularly. I was torn between thoroughly enjoying his company and wanting to jam a couple of plugs up his nose while he was fast asleep. His personality was splintering into two, and the evil twin was winning. One minute I was whipping up a meal with him, and the next minute he'd boot me out of the kitchen for no obvious reason.

Cabin fever moved through the boat, grabbing hold of the guys and making them uptight and irrational. Trapped in a drifting daytime melodrama, I took the role of audience member during breaks in the action and wondered what would happen next to the poor observer. I became the fiction in their friction. Maybe this was the point the female observer on our sister ship had reached.

The next episode came all too soon.

Storyteller Wade, Ed, Cool Boy, Tito, and I had been on deck painting the vessel's Fish and Game identification number in dark blue paint on the pink buoys. Now it was cookie prep time, and I entered the food supply room alone, or so I thought. I scaled the ceiling-high shelving unit like scaffolding and strained to reach two bags of chocolate chips on the top shelf. Then I heard an excited, "N*iii*ce!" and felt teeth sinking fast and furious into the back of my Levi's. With me in them.

Shocked, I yelled, "What the . . . ?" Then I dropped the chocolate, teetered on the shelf edge, and launched a roundhouse blow with the accuracy of a kickboxer. I fell to the floor, pain shooting up through my shins, and faced the predator.

Unbelievable. Hobey, the bottom-feeder catfish. The mate! This was taking his label as a free spirit to a whole new level.

I grabbed him by the neck and growled, "Who do you think you are, you little moron?" I wanted to bat him like a whiffle ball, but instead whacked the baseball cap off his head. This was no flirty tug of the ponytail on the playground. He bit me in the butt! I really wanted to take him down.

"If you *ever* again come close to touching me *anywhere,* I will beat the shinola out of you!"

Half giggling, he said, "Oh, I'm sorry. I got a little carried away. I was just goofing around." His eyes begged forgiveness, but could I? What possessed him to do such a thing, and what kind of reaction did he expect from me? And then, who would I tell? Captain Gus? He was preparing to make me even more miserable.

A week later, I stood silent behind Captain Gus in the wheelhouse with my face out the window tallying the catch for two hours. Click, click, click, my frozen fingers keeping count with the clicker. His cigarette smoke swirled through the wheelhouse. Tally—five, ten, fifteen-plus cod—with a pencil on my white-board. Guns N' Roses or Metallica screeched in the background, drowning out the whine of the gear and the calls of the gulls flying beside the vessel.

After my haul tally was complete, I headed down the stairs to finish my sampling in the factory. Captain Killjoy summoned me back to the wheelhouse with a yell, "Hey, Laura, get back here."

"What's up, Gus?"

"Laura, you are no longer allowed to help cook in the galley." He looked hard at the instruments, his brows pointed at right angles.

I snickered to displace some of the heavy air. This had to be some sick joke. "Too many compliments on my daily batches of homemade cookies? No, no. Let me guess. My grandma's Polish sauerkraut and kielbasa recipe gave everyone gas?"

Frowning, he said, "I'm not joking. It's a company decision based on safety and liability."

He pulled his eyes away from the horizon and looked straight at me. I scanned for the black spot in his eye and saw a cold, dark tunnel.

I raised my voice. "What? You're banning me from cooking? Come on. That's ridiculous! I've been helping Jazz for seventy-three days straight! I've been cooking since age nine!" I could use Captain Gabe in my corner right now; I needed him to swear for me. I wanted to hear, "Miss Snacky Cakes, Gus is *such* an *asshole*."

Who had ignited this flame? Jazz the cook? Hobey the mate? I had no idea, and Captain Killjoy wasn't going to tell me.

I didn't confess to Gus how I'd been helping the crew this whole time—cutting gangions off line with serrated deck knives, splicing line, and tying on pointy barbed hooks. I'd also filleted fish and gave another whirl at welding with the Chief engineer. He thought my handling hot pans in the galley was dangerous? He was serious;

I could no longer bake, roast, fry, boil, chop, or flip a spatula in the galley. He took away my last small joy and tiny bit of freedom.

The grand finale came within a week. It was after midnight, and I had finished sampling. Before heading to bed, I went into the factory stern with three cups of hot chocolate to deliver it to a few crewmen. Immediately, the skunky scent of marijuana pushed out the briny air and turned my stomach sour. Some of the crew lit up often. I also heard rumors about the occasional use of cocaine, but if it was true they'd kept it hidden from my sight. In the crew's eyes, I was fully playful, halfway mischievous and a quarter goodie-goodie who never sought to drink, smoke, or do drugs. Some of the crew, with their pupils dilated like high beams, humdrum attitudes, and slow reactions, made me consider our safety. Seconds mattered in this environment. Still, I didn't infringe on what the guys did; everybody was different. It was their business. My business was fish, the catch. I didn't bother bringing it to the attention of Captain Gus. He would just say I shouldn't be in the factory outside of sampling in the first place and likely ban me from there as well. I liked hanging out with many of the guys and feared my time with them might be reduced to quarantined conversations at mealtime in the galley. I certainly didn't want that.

I bounced into the gear overhaul area in the stern of the factory like Tigger ready to pounce and play with his animal friends.

"Who's ready for some hot chocolate?" I asked. I handed the mugs off, but the usual round of thanks was missing, and they looked at me stone-faced. Something was up. I turned around and there, on the freshly painted white wall like a billboard hung the centerfold from a porn magazine with "OBSERVER" written above it in black marker. My heart sank. Is that what they thought about me?

I was crushed more than I'd ever been. Why didn't a few good guys, those I was there to help and work alongside, defend me and rip it off the wall? Captain Gabe's daily repetition of "All men are pigs" ballooned in my head, and I felt his absence. I could take a lot of their false stories, snarky remarks, suspicious looks, and even a raw bite in the butt, but this time I was speechless. It seemed the gang had turned on me.

I recoiled, holding back the tears, and stormed out of the factory. I tore off my heavy overalls and boots, slammed them down hard against the dryer, and ran to the thin protection of my dark bunk. I curled up in my sleeping bag, rolling with the heavy waves, and broke down. The crew wasn't satisfied until they made the tough girl cry. Well, they'd finally succeeded. I bawled silently, trying not to wake Cool Boy. I couldn't even cry out loud, alone.

I covered my head to deepen the darkness, and for the first time understood how placing a pillow over her head had comforted my Mom in her despair, when the thin veil of closed eyelids wasn't enough. I can only suppose this is how she felt, under a barrage of attacks, leaving her defenseless and too weak to face the day.

What had convinced me that working on a fishing boat was a good idea? I needed someone to tell me I wasn't crazy for being uncomfortable with strange men walking around in their underwear, peeing in front of me, and referring to me with pictures from porn magazines. I'd reached my max. I needed a long break from the guys, but I still had weeks remaining in my contract, and this trip could run longer. I'd tried to be fun, open, positive, and hardworking, but still some of the guys would never treat me as their equal or respect me. They viewed me beneath the Bering Sea burka as *that* girl spread-eagle on the poster.

I partially blamed Captain Gus, who set the negative tone of the boat. If I'd told him about the homebrew, the bite in the butt, the crew smoking pot, the porn pinup, or any other issues, he would consider me a troublemaker, a whiner, an oversensitive female on counter-attack after my kitchen eviction. He'd never side with me. I felt betrayed and brimmed with distrust; I needed a friend, a shoulder to cry on, a listening ear, or at least a sincere hug. Something.

The next morning Russell, who had been on his sleep shift and missed the incident in the stern, stopped me in the hallway.

"You okay? I heard what the guys did to you last night," he whispered. "I'm sorry. It's not right."

"Yeah, *not* cool. They're awful," I said, feeling vulnerable.

"They think you're beautiful and all of 'em have a crush on you," he said, trying to explain their behavior. "They're in competition with each other and frustrated because you won't give in to any of them."

I had an idea. "Ya know, Russell, I found a spot for us to hang out. It's the gear storage locker on the aft deck. Why don't you meet me there after dinner is over? I'd like to chat in private."

"Sure. Whatever you want. I'll be there."

Whatever I want? Well, maybe it was time I did give in to their stories. They would find out about our secret meeting, as nothing is secret in the confines of a fishing vessel. Gossip would come out of this, but this time I wouldn't let it bother me.

What did I want to talk about anyway? It reminded me of a conversation with Mom when I was in high school. I had a Tom Selleck poster plastered on the ceiling above my bed. Mom was amused by my crush on this mature man rather than boys my age.

"What would you do if you had him?" she asked.

"I have no idea, but I'd figure it out."

I told myself the same about my invitation to Russell. We'd just talk. In the dark. In a confined space. Away from the weather, and the men.

Most of the crew got the cues that my tolerance for nonsense had flat-lined, so I thought they'd behave better. Until lunch. I walked into the galley to see Juan, the crewman with silken skin and a gap between his front teeth. The day before on the aft deck he'd said to me with his thick Mexican accent, "Your *sweee*per is down."

"My what?" Frustrated, I raised my voice. "What the heck is a sweeper?"

"Your *sweee*per!" He said, pointing to my zipper.

Many times in the past he had offered, "Can I teach you some salsa moves . . ." Which I would have gladly welcomed, if he had not ended the offer with ". . . or somethe*ee*ng else?"

I'd already had enough of him this day. At breakfast he kept pointing at the mound of cooked sausages in the warming tray and repeated, "Laura, *el burro, el burro*," referring to a donkey's penis, I suppose. He got a lot of laughs, but still stunned from the girly poster on the wall the night before, I went from lighthearted to heavyhearted.

Now I was in the galley waiting for lunch to be ready and enjoying the *In Living Color* episodes playing back-to-back on the VCR. Then I had that someone-is-watching-me vibe. By the expressions on the crewmen's faces, my instincts were correct. I whipped around to see Juan right behind me, grinning ear-to-ear, biting his lower lip, and humping the air with a few pelvic thrusts to arouse his audience.

I *snapped*.

My mind reverted to Mom's self-defense lessons. "Kick him in the nuts!" and "Go for the throat like a wild animal," she'd instructed.

In a knee-jerk reaction, I twisted around and heaved my fist into his stomach. He doubled over and fell to the linoleum floor. Lying sideways and clutching his chest, he gasped in his slow, slurred accent without breath. "Why-d-j*oo* do that? I can *loook* if I don't *touch*."

I was surprised by my knee-jerk reaction, and worried he might get up and throw a Mexican hook to my liver. Standing over him,

I shook my fist over his face, his bandana now half hanging off his head, and said, "If you gawk at me anymore you'll be right back down on the floor again, you piece of crap! Next time it'll be in your *el burro*!"

I'd never gut-punched the wind out of anyone before, and I never wanted to do it again. Juan and his fans lost their sly smiles and sat silent. I unclenched my fist and my teeth. Maybe they'd let up a little on me now.

That night I went to the storage locker and left the heavy door cracked open several inches and burrowed myself into the cylinders of line. Russell and I had looked directly at each other after dinner, signaling the plan was on. Now I was just waiting to see his fingers curl around the door.

The ship rolled and twisted. The springy coils were becoming harder and more frozen beneath me. As I waited, I prayed silently: for my family to be happy, for a stable career on land, for the seemingly impossible true love. I also prayed for the guys aboard to mellow, and if they didn't, for me to chill out and react better.

The door cracked open. "Is there room for two in there?" Russell asked.

He rearranged a few heavy bundles to separate us from the cold metal wall. In the dark except for the light from the moon reflecting off the water, we sat bundled side by side, warmed by each other. We talked, truly alone for the first time. We both confessed that we had love interests back on land. He had plans to end his, where I hoped mine would have a new start. We removed our wool gloves and held hands like sixth-graders.

In a quiet moment, between his encouragement and my nervous laughter, he said, "I still want to give you a birthday kiss."

"Russell, that's not why I invited you here." I squirmed, putting a few more inches between us. "I don't think that's such a good..."

It was too late. His cologne and his arms engulfed me.

The hardships endured during this last trip, especially the past few days, were instantly eased. All I had needed was a hug, but this was the giant release of held breaths from an attraction that had been building for months.

I pulled away from his heat.

"I knew you'd be a good kisser," he said, coaxing me back into his strong arms.

"Russell, as much as I want more of you, we can't meet like this again. We have to remain in the "just friends" category until we're off the boat. There's been too much gossip already, and now they actually have something to talk about."

"That's cool. I understand." He warmed my bare hand in his calloused palm. We leaned back in toward each other, providing some comfort to our Bering Sea struggles.

We talked for a while, and then left the love nest separately to avoid being spotted together, although the crew no doubt already knew. Back in my stateroom, I crawled into my bunk in the dark, biting my lip to hide the smile from my face. Jazz was snoring in the bottom bunk, stopping when my knee hit the sidewall. I turned on my light and could dimly see that Underwear Man's curtain was drawn shut. Cool Boy was working his shift in the factory. My dive watch glowed, showing that an hour had passed quickly in the locker. I moved my pillow so I could wiggle into my sleeping bag and saw a loose ball of toilet paper. I unwrapped the layers to find a Snickers bar. A kind gesture toward the beaten down observer? A conciliatory gift, I hoped. Amends accepted.

The weeks went on and the guys' behavior improved. We watched movies in the galley, laughed together, played cards, and made little bets as we had done in the past. Camaraderie was back in full force. Now the guys, even Juan, joked about my sucker punch, saying things like, "Don't mess with Laura. She's from Chicago and will flatten you." Even the way Underwear Man looked at me changed. Better still, not one word was uttered about my rendez-vous with Russell. Maybe we'd all reached the point of exhaustion, an acceptance of our faults and our fates at sea. No one ever fessed up to leaving the Snickers bar either. Maybe I'd finally completed the hazing and had been initiated into this crew.

I'd been worn down and was probably oversensitive at times. I had to step back and put my sea life in perspective. I'm sure other observers endured similar situations. Later, Stef would tell me about a female observer on a six-man catcher boat who had relayed the official secret SOS code to NMFS that's only to be used in a life-threatening situation. (Technically, SOS is a morse code, invented by Samuel Morse, which means "Save our Ship" or "Save our Souls." It replaced the formerly used CQD code, "All stations. Distress.") After the observer sent the secret code to Seattle, the Coast Guard immediately ordered her ship back to town.

That emergency turned into a charge of sexual harassment. Later the truth was uncovered: the observer had spent her days locked in her room, because she refused the crew's request for her to help wash dishes. It's common for fishermen to have multiple duties on smaller vessels and, although it's not required, it's a wel-comed courtesy for observers to assist with the daily chores. The crew claimed the observer was lazy and had a bad attitude. She stated that she wasn't required to work outside of her job descrip-tion. Ironically, I felt spited on my boat knowing other smaller ships would've likely welcomed my help and my chocolate chip cookies.

Granted, some of the actions of the men I worked alongside—Underwear Man, Hobey, Captain Gus, and Juan—were blatantly awful, so I had reason to dislike them. Still, I never thought to send out the SOS. What constituted a life-threatening situation? Sexual advances? A crew stoned on marijuana or under the influence of bad grape homebrew? A bite on the butt? I didn't welcome any of these, but I never felt seriously threatened. None of we female observers were clear on what was appropriate and at what level to react. We just figured it out and drew our boundaries in the air. For me to thrive for the rest of my contract, I had to view the odd gossip and some of the hard-to-handle guys as a nuisance, a job hazard. I wouldn't magnify the trouble and squelch the good. I sucked up and chalked up the misdemeanors to being on a boat full of dudes. Maybe this was another series of lessons in forgiving others and even my imperfect self during the times we when least deserved it. It was time to pull together and cling to the good guys aboard. To me, there were bigger, more real dangers than men behaving badly.

16

MUTINY

WHILE sampling a few days after the summer solstice, I chucked one nine- to fifteen-pound black cod after the next into my swinging blue basket. Suddenly, a wave of commotion rippled through the factory to the bow. Something bad had happened, again, which I'd learned wasn't so unusual on a commercial fishing boat. Dangers were always high. Still, with each alarm my body tensed. I held my breath and pulled from a long list of worst-case scenarios. Engine failure? We're sinking and my survival suit is upstairs in my bunk? Man overboard? Someone is hurt? Yes, this time it was Josef, the young Czechoslovakian with the ponytails. He popped a hernia lifting a quarter-tote of coiled line.

Selfishly, my first thoughts chimed with celebration. I didn't think too much about poor Josef with his guts squeezing out his body like air from a pierced inner tube. I thought: Our sister ship can deliver us toilet paper at sea, but they weren't going to solve the problem this time by bringing us a doctor. I threw a fist pump in the air, followed by a two-handed "raise the roof." This was it. This was my good news, despite his bad news. Surely, we were heading back to port, probably for my last time. At this point, I doubted the office would send me on another long trip. My contract would technically be up at ninety days; it was day eighty-four. Gangway! Only a few days of steaming 600 miles east and we'd be in the promised land of Dutch Harbor. I would be Seattle bound. Woo-hoo!

Through the many crises we endured, I learned how to react by reading the crew's faces, and the guys' expressions didn't share my same excitement. Why weren't they in full celebration? I conferred with Daniel the Irishman, who always seemed to be in the know, "I hear Josef is hurt. It sounds bad. We're headed home, right?"

"No, I doubt it. Not yet." He pulled his cap down over his tawny curls. "My money is on Am*shit*ka, Amchitka Island."

"What? Amchitka? Where's that? We're not going to Dutch? We're not going home? He needs a doctor." I felt like I was on a flight for a beach vacation and the plane was diverted to another airport. Observer Girl had once again falsely rung the bell of hope.

Amchitka Island is one of the Rat Islands that housed a naval air facility and the nearest available medical help—good for Josef, bad for the rest of us. The base was built in 1943 as preparation for the US invasion of the two Japanese-occupied Western Aleutian Islands, Attu and Kiska, and the northern islands of Japan. In the late 1980s, a US long-range surveillance system was constructed on the island to track aircraft and ships up to 2,500 nautical miles off the US coastline. It was also used to survey the Russian coastline and had shut down only a few months before we docked there. Similar systems were still being used in other parts of the country for counter-narcotics surveillance and early warning systems for the military. Amchitka had served as a military outpost, a radio range station, a weather monitoring post for Russia, and now an alternate landing site in the Aleutians to kick injured crew to the curb.

"He's good people," Ed said, nudging me with his elbow. "Laura, you don't wanna sample the fish around Amchitka. They glow in the dark. Huh, huh, huh."

The US Department of Defense and the Atomic Energy Commission fired underground nuclear test detonations there between 1965 and 1971. The blasts caused radioactive contamination of deep groundwater that could transfer to seawater and sediment and up the marine food chain to wildlife and humans. Direct contact with surface water was potentially hazardous to humans.

As we docked there, I wondered why my sampling gear didn't include a Geiger counter. Josef was transported to the expiring base, located somewhere on the desolate forty-mile-long strip.

While waiting to hear about the severity of Josef's injury, most of us braved the forty mph winds to use the single phone booth rising out of the earth like a misplaced monolith. With the temperature just above freezing, the cool rain and whirlwind gusts united the crew and me into a huddle, standing in line shivering like Arctic penguins. Still, we welcomed any chance to get off the ship, and the earth felt good beneath our boots. When it was my turn, no one answered my calls, and my lips were too numb to say much, so I left brief messages on answering machines. If they could see me now: ankle deep in toxic mud, a wind-chapped face, and sweatpants soaked to my skin just for the chance to hear their voices.

We got an update on Josef's status: critical. He required immediate surgery. Though he'd toughened up over the past few months, I wondered about his state of mind. Was he nervous being away from his captain and shipmates? Maybe he was happy to be done fishing and getting off the boat. Or maybe because he was unable to fish any longer due to his injury he'd have to return to the Czech Republic and suffer lost wages or loss of a job. Maybe he'd try to sue the fishing company for fault, as many fishermen do when they're injured. Regardless, we left him behind on the island. I thought

Dutch Harbor was a ghost town until I hit eerie Amchitka. I'd just seen a whole lot of nothing, but nothing on land had been a welcomed break to nothing at sea. I scraped the gooey sludge off my boots on the lipped edge of the deck as I reboarded and hoped it wasn't *too* contaminated.

We pushed off Amchitka, an island brutalized by weather and military history, now on the mend as an Alaska Maritime National Wildlife Refuge, housing more sea lions than people. The harsh outline of the island evoked in me the words of Albert Einstein, "There are two ways to live your life. One is as though nothing is a miracle. The other is as if everything is." It was miraculous any life form could survive such severe conditions. A Midwestern girl making it to Alaska and surviving on a fishing boat in the middle of the Bering Sea, enveloped by rugged nature and extreme weather few ever witness, also seemed miraculous.

After eighty-four long days afloat with only a turn and burn offload in Dutch and a medical stop in Amchitka, I needed Seattle. But I wasn't going to get it yet. I pictured Captain Gus with a gaff at my back like a pirate sword yelling, "Stay out of the galley, Laura. There will be no fun and certainly no cookie baking while I'm Captain. Walk the plank or join the crew!"

Maybe we would continue to fish until the crew lost their minds and started migrating en masse across the sea like lemmings in search of new habitat. Our desperation and desire to go home built with each passing hour.

As a storm powered up, so surged the swear words from the mouths of the men: "This fucking sucks!" It pulled them all together.

The CPU (catch per unit) of sablefish and turbot catch was poor, which meant the guys did nearly the same amount of work without making any money. With only about five days worth of fuel remaining, we began to process just about every piece of spare change (low-value fish) that came up on the line: idiot fish, arrowtooth flounder and even skate wings. We scrambled to pack on as much product as possible.

Due to the bad weather and our fishing location near a jagged reef, we had lost about three miles of gear in twenty-four hours. Since we caught more snarled loops of line and twisted gangions than fish, the more time was spent unwinding, repairing, and recoiling the gear. The crew thought it senseless to continue fishing and wanted to quit, to motor back to port. *Vámonos!* But the office in Seattle ruled: Keep fishing. I expected mutiny, and I would stand in solidarity with the crew.

Captain Gus had heard over the radio that two guys were stabbed to death in Dutch Harbor and thrown into the bay, as if that were defense to stay out of port. I wondered if it happened at the Elbow Room, still living up to its reputation as the roughest bar in America. I still wanted to visit.

Gus ordered the crew to soak a few more sets. When you've been at sea so long, what difference did a few more sets make anyway? It felt like torture. The deckhands had had enough. In retaliation, they began to "part the line with deck knives," slaying it like an evil deep-sea dragon. with deck knives. Left to their devices, we would run out of gear before we could possibly run out of fuel, and we'd be forced back into town. If that didn't work, maybe they'd start throwing our dwindled food supply overboard. We knew we needed a bigger crisis than a shortage of toilet paper or a critical injury to go back home; and they were prepared to create one.

For days the weather gave us a real wallop, beating us and our catch down hard. Though storms were usually viewed as our enemy, the oncoming hurricane-force winds became our welcomed rescue. Captain Gus made the announcement: "It's too nasty to keep fishing and we have too little fuel for backup. Pull the gear."

We set our evacuation route toward Dutch Harbor and were scheduled to hit dock the next day.

That night, unable to sleep, I laid in my bunk listening to sultry John Coltrane ballads. My emotions matched the up and down of each crescendo and crashing wave. Above all, I wanted to leave this roller coaster and hop on a plane homeward, but what came next? Most of the guys were ecstatic, talking of their spouses, girlfriends, and families. It made me a bit envious. I would be returning to my studio apartment, where my plants were the only (hopefully) living things waiting for me.

There was also the chance of rekindling the relationship with Luke. I wondered if his heart—which he'd poured out in his let-ters—and arms were still open and ready to welcome me.

This was my last night on the high seas curled up next to my survival suit, sleeping on a wooden shelf above snoring Jazz. I could hardly believe I'd been at sea for three long months. What would life on land be like after this? The smooth tenor saxophone lulled me to sleep at last.

My zeal returned the next day when I woke up to Cool Boy's morning greeting: "Laura, LaURA, LAURA. Guess what? The sun is shining, and we'll be in port tonight!"

Soon I'd be back to sleeping in my own bed and other daily sim-plicities that now seemed indulgent: ringing telephones, a bathtub, shaving my legs, and wearing makeup and jewelry. I would leave behind my well-worn jeans and sweats like a snake's cast-off skin. At last I could wear something that wasn't saggy and baggy. I would wash my own laundry, cook my own food and bake in my own tiny kitchen where the appliances aren't bolted down. I was finally going home.

Blessed with clear skies and a warm breeze, the crew came alive like horses heading back to the barn after a long ride. Though many of the processors had to spend their time cleaning smashed fish bodies out of the metal grates and equipment, several deckhands, including Russell, untied the pink buoys from the railing and we jumped around on them like kindergarten cowboys on Hippity Hops. Now, none of the past resentments and frustrating moments seemed to matter. The playfulness reminded me of our trip under Captain Gabe's watch.

In hindsight, I attributed the bad behavior to what Captain Gabe had told me when I'd asked: "Why do a group of men lose their minds when a woman is around?"

"We have to first get your attention so we can rival for you, and then find interesting ways to keep your attention. We're like male baboons, where the competition comes down to who has the reddest ass, a contest I would probably win. The men who didn't suffer manically from this compulsion fell out of the gene pool a long time ago. We're the ones who made it."

Beneath the crew's tough and tense exteriors were souls that harbored similar worries as mine. Stuck at sea while we were all trying to build a stronger foundation for ourselves back on land. I wish I'd had the maturity then to dig deeper into each of their life stories and then maybe I would have better understood their perspectives. I would miss this zany crew and *some* of their fisher-manly ways.

Russell was staying behind on the vessel for another trip or two. I wondered if I'd see him again back in Seattle. What would it be like to really talk to him freely, away from staring eyes and soap opera story lines?

After three months on Alaska's high seas, I packed away my Army jacket and put on the "crew jacket" given to me by Captain Gabe. I spent my final moments onboard not hidden in the storage locker but lying across coiled line piled into fish totes under open sky, a brilliant sun, and soothing wind. A pod of Dall's porpoise playfully splashed alongside the ship. Nothing could erase my smile. Twelve miles away, a steaming, snow-capped volcano peaked out from high clouds. The start of summer in Seattle, while in

Alaska the first shoots were just now emerging through the thawing earth. The fifty-degree wind on my skin felt warm after the harsh Bering Sea spring. The sun coaxed me out of isolation and drew me closer to my mysterious future—the future I told myself I should welcome. I wanted to freeze-frame the moment and etch it in my memory forever. Hope had brought me here—hope that originated on the shores of Lake Michigan, stretching beyond the waters of Table Rock Lake in the Ozarks to Seattle's Puget Sound, and finally reaching the Bering Sea. I paused to take in the magnificence and peace around me—a last deep breath before you pass from one realm to the next.

17

~~~~

BERING SEA PTSD (POST-TRAUMATIC SEA DISORDER)

A twilight touchdown at SeaTac airport slammed me back into land life and sensory overload: people, stores, lights, and chatter blaring over intercoms. Most travelers around me had returned from a vacation; I had been brought back from another dimension. My senses were heightened in Alaska, and now the noise of our everyday lives sounded like candy Pop Rocks in my mouth. The shuttle van hurried through turns with abrupt starts and stops and darted around vehicles, unlike the steady roll of waves beneath the ship. I felt jittery, seasick—no, carsick. Headlights and lamp-posts shined like lasers. The city shrieked. I'd been gone for three months, all of spring, but it seemed much longer. I'd missed out on the transition into a new season, the lush scents and sights of nature waking up from its winter slumber: rain soaking into soil, tree buds breaking open, hyacinths unfurling, and freshly cut grass. I felt far-removed in this place and expected it might take some time to readjust.

The Space Needle, towering above like a giant lighthouse, guided me back to the curb of my brick apartment building—my safe harbor. I looked to the spot where Lucas helped me with my license plates. "Never give up," he'd told me before speeding away in his shopping cart. I wondered what had happened in his life while I was gone, and if the blanket I'd given him had helped keep him warm at night. I wheeled my baskets of gear—the eighty-pound, government-issued ball and chain—down the red-carpeted hallway to studio 403. I cracked open the door feeling like an intruder in my own place. The 550 square feet, though stuffy, seemed more spacious and comfortable than I remembered. I cast aside the remnants of my Bering Sea life into a heap on the floor. Brown leaves dropped from my plants. My "view"—the five blocks of rooftops and concrete between me and the brackish waters of Puget Sound—no longer seemed worthy of my awe. Gone was my 360-degree unobstructed view of nothing but surging ocean, open sky, and whales I could almost touch. For three months, I had longed for this, for civilization. Now, standing in my apartment, I realized the magnitude of the natural beauty I'd been immersed in at sea.

I pressed play on my answering machine and heard the recording I'd left before leaving for Alaska: "Hi! You've reached Laura. I'm gone fishing. Leave a message." I listened to several welcome home voicemails. I thought about picking up the phone to return the calls, but I couldn't. It took too much energy. I was too tired with too much to tell, so I didn't phone anyone, not a friend, not my family.

I laid down, soaking in the luxury of my plush twin mattress on the floor. There were no clothes or survival suit stuffed beneath it. No walls to hold me in place. No need for a blue curtain strung to protect my privacy. No more male roommates to tiptoe around or plug my ears to silence their snores. No one to leave the toilet seat up. No sounds of grinding gear. No more haulback-wakeup-shake-downs from Jazz. No more anchor time. No hanging my cold face out the window or frigid fingers on clicker-counters. No flinging, slinging, slicing, measuring, or weighing fish. No washing myself down with a fire hose. My at-sea work was officially done.

I closed my eyes, and was surprised by the boatload of tears welling up. My mind wanted to switch back to land, but my body was still at sea. I couldn't let go of the vivid ocean swell and the slow roll of the ship beneath me. I already missed the crashing waves, the howling and shifting winds, with the sound of seagulls echoing in the background. This first night back in my Seattle apartment felt as foreign as the sea had felt to me that first day I boarded my vessel. I wasn't sure I wanted to be here.

Where else could I go? Where was home, if not here? Home used to mean family, but my family had slowly disintegrated and scattered like dust. Just like the past months spent at sea, some-times it's hard to see your reality until it's in your wake. I had three months to think about my childhood, my life. I thought back to the incident with the gun between my brother and mom the year before. That last affirming push out of the Ozarks seemed like so long ago.

My mom and brother both seemed to lack the ability to cope, to self-soothe, to find the right words to express themselves rather than yell. They self-destructed, medicated, held in what bothered them, and then pushed it outward with full force into their cruel world and onto others, especially those they loved. How much was attributable to bad behavior, to disability, to chemical imbalance, or to plain lack of self-control? And would it ever change?

What was it like to be my mother, boiling over like a hot kettle left on the stove until her insides burned dry and sooty. From what did the anger stem, and could she ever release enough of it to set herself free? Since I was a child, her comfort seemed to be behind closed doors, dark shades and eye masks, pillows and blankets over her head.

What was it like to live in my brother's shoes? Due to his disability and by no fault of his own, he was stuck in adolescence and driven by impulse. He was a direct product of his upbringing, but had little capacity to think his way out of problems or bad decisions or to protect his fragile, boyish heart. He was frustrated, trying to figure out how to be a man, but was ill equipped.

For them life was too intense, the average day's crises too overwhelming. We each chose differently within our own capacity and found ways to mask our pains, disappointments, and losses we hadn't yet fully grieved. Mom turned to her anger, dark rooms, and medications. Tom resorted to drinking. I prayed to God and hit the throttle west, winding up on the Bering Sea.

I grabbed two of the last letters I had received in Dutch Harbor. The one from Mom said, "I'm trying real hard to change my negatives into positives. It's probably the hardest thing I've ever had to do."

My brother had signed a sweet card with his honest and vulnerable heart, "Love, your stupid brother, Tom." Both made me cry. My family wasn't the sole reason for my leaving Missouri, but still a case for not yet going back.

On my first full day back in Seattle, I slowly began to break the mental barrier between Alaskan boat life and Seattle city life. I tidied up my paperwork so I could begin the long NMFS debriefing process. Stephanie was already in the midst of it. Debriefing could take more than two weeks, depending on how many vessels and fisheries an observer had been assigned, the diversity of their catches, and how error-free our data sheets were.

At NMFS, a female debriefer verified my sampling methods and conducted an exit survey. She asked, "Do you have any reports of dangerous incidents, sexual harassment, illegal possession of prohibited species, violations, or safety issues?"

She checked the boxes as I answered, "Hmm, no. I don't have anything worth reporting. Just normal, everyday fishing boat life I guess."

On the wall of her cubicle, I noticed several photos of her and a guy embracing on the deck of fishing boat.

"Who's that?" I asked. "A friend? A brother?"

"Husband," she responded. "I met him years ago when I was an observer on a trawler. He was one of the deckhands." She circled one of my catch totals and drew a red line through a few of my numbers.

"Husband? *Really*? But I thought love connections between observers and fishermen were frowned upon. Ya know, allegedly illegal?"

"Ohhh, yes," she said in a hushed tone. "They are, but I'd say about a quarter of us were or are involved with fishermen."

Suddenly, I didn't feel so alone and so wrong about my at-sea crush on Russell. I appreciated her honesty and could finally stop punishing myself for the push and pull of the temptations at sea.

Within days of our return, Stef and I were lying on a Puget Sound cobble beach coated with inches of imported Hawaiian sand. Both of us relaxed deeply. The Seattle summer sun ripening my skin like an olive, while Stef's went from white to pink. Though we hadn't seen each other or talked for months, our friendship had flourished through letters while at sea. We survived our journeys apart, but we had been united the whole time.

We stood and linked arms, then counted—One. Two. Three!—before plunging into Puget Sound. The fifty-three-degree water stabbed our skin, but the swim satisfied our need for a bit of vacation paradise, far from the icy Bering Sea.

Life wasn't pushing us in any one direction, but our time in Alaska had filled us with vigor and confidence, and we believed we could achieve anything if we set our minds on it.

As we laid on the beach, two guys approached. The absence of flannel, fish-stained sweatshirts, baggy sweatpants with Dutch Harbor written down the leg, tall rubber boots, and orange rain gear, left their large pecs in full view—a view I would soak in without guilt.

"Hello, ladies," said the one with a football tucked under his bicep. "How ya' doing today? You look like athletes. Wanna throw the ball around?"

Tempting, really. But I looked at Stef and then back at the beau hunks. "Um. You have no idea what we've just been through." It was obvious they were caught off guard. My reaction surprised me, too. Normally I would've generously helped them with their tanning oil. But this time, all I could think was—Stop! Halt! "Sorry. I just got off a fishing boat in the Bering Sea a couple days ago. Me and twenty-five guys for ninety days straight," I explained. "Not to be rude, but, honestly, we're not interested."

Intrigued, they moved in closer wanting to hear more. I chilled out, wondering if I had misspoken for Stef. She had broken up with her boyfriend back home and might want to get to know one or both of these guys.

But with arms crossed, Stephanie stepped in with a similar retort, "Fifty men, eighty-five days." They walked off, eyeing us like we were aliens. They couldn't understand that we had our fill of men for a while and had a strong case of Bering Sea PTSD (Post-Traumatic Sea Disorder). For now we had a lot of catching up to do, and no one messed with girl time. Men weren't allowed . . . at least not yet.

18

~~

GIRL TIME

BETWEEN our debriefings, Stephanie and I spent our free time shopping and indulging in luxuries we had missed during our time at sea. We bought everything new, right down to our underwear. During our shopping trip, I realized that I felt different—I *was* different.

Before life at sea, I thought of myself as just one of the guys, most comfortable in rugged outdoor-wear and boots, until I lived with them for ninety days straight. I finally noticed what others had been telling me for years: I possessed a feminine side. They say a boy leaves for the military and returns a man. Well, the Bering Sea turned this tomboy into a whole lotta woman.

At sea the work validated me: my intelligence, a strong and resilient body, and the wide breadth of my character. I learned my femininity wasn't appearance based, used as a tool to gain men's attention or affection, but rather an inherent and significant part of me. I would no longer conceal, downplay, or apologize for my outward appearance as if masking a handicap. I didn't need the baggy clothes, the Bering Sea burka, to hide my feminine energy and sexuality in order to appear strong or smart. The Bering Sea taught me I was more capable than I'd realized. Now I wanted to be recognized and valued for all parts of me, beyond the social constructs and stereotypes placed on women. I now see my feminine side as a strength.

Because I was deprived of all things female at sea, I discovered the woman confined within me. More often now, I removed the baseball hat, pulled down the ponytail and added a few curls to my long hair. I traded out my *plannels* (plaid flannels) for floral prints or tailored stripes, shapeless baggy Chinos for slim-fitting pants, and clunky boots that hid my ankles for strappy, open-toed heels that exposed my hot pink nail polish. My go-to colors switched from brown, grey, and black winter earth tones, or "colors of death and doom" as Mom called them, to bright colors, the kind that attract bees, hummingbirds, and men's smiles. However, pastels still had no place in my closet.

I developed a strong desire to wear lipstick, the frosted kind, and dresses above the knee, though typically I hadn't worn much of either. I craved makeup, hair goo, perfume and scented lotions, smooth legs, and outfits that couldn't be traded with the guys. Though I still missed my Chicago sweatshirt I had lost to Jazz and would never completely let go of T-shirts and athletic wear, I would wear my true size and not hide my figure.

While Stef and I browsed, we shared the bests of the Bering Sea, along with some of the worsts.

"Laura, I never want to get a whiff of anything that disgusting again," she said while trying on a black pump at Nordstrom's. "I smelled it before I even saw it."

Stef had been assigned to a trawler that fished with a net. It pulled up over forty tons of fish at once and dumped it through open hatches on deck into holding tanks below in the factory. There, the catch was released through a small door near the bottom of the tank in a controlled stream onto a conveyor belt for processing.

"So, what was the smell from? What was it?" I asked, bracing myself for any response.

"I didn't know at first. It was a big gray blob of rotting flesh."

"No! Gross! Was it a sea lion?" Besides sinking, pulling up a sea lion was one of our biggest fears as observers because of what we'd have to do next.

"Yes! A sea lion. But worse, it jammed up the tank door, so the guys had to jump into the tank from the above deck with fire axes and hack up the body. That thing splattered all over. I held my breath and tried to get a look at it while they moved the slabs away from the door. I thought, I still have to chop its nose off to recover the teeth so the lab can estimate its age."

"Oh, my gosh, Stef. I'm going to puke just thinking about it. Did you do it? Did you saw off its snout?" I stood in disgust, unbalanced wearing one pink kitten heel and one white sandal.

"Well, when I got close, it was headless! It had already rotted off and been devoured by sand fleas before we'd caught it."

The whole story made me want to scrub down in a hot shower.

I tossed her another pair of sassy heels. "Stef, we've only been home for a couple weeks, and I still can't fathom it. Our observer days at sea were bizarre: dangerous weather, unstable crew members, hacking up reeking mammal bodies, and slicing up codfish bellies." It was all so unreal.

"Ya wanna hear something crazy?" Stef asked as she grabbed my shoulder (probably to hold herself up for making such a decision). "I've decided to sign up for another three-month contract."

"No way. You can't. What about our exotic gal pal trip to a tropical paradise to thaw out our bones?"

Throughout observer training, I'd made big plans for us to travel together before we got real jobs on land. She never fully committed. It was my dream, not hers, but I'd hoped our frozen months at sea would convince her to go.

"Girlfriend, go to Alaska with me," Stef said. "Maybe then we can go on a trip. Plus, think of how many pairs of shoes we can buy afterwards."

"Think of how many sea lion snouts we might have to chop off for those shoes," I retorted.

Like me, she had little to stay home for—no job and no future plans. Was *Muy Picante* Ben, her deckhand crush, behind her decision? Should I also take a chance at love and move to Florida to be near Luke? My mind swung between coasts, from tropical beaches to icy oceans. Why should I stay in Seattle? Why not go to Florida? Or heck, back to Alaska?

My immediate goals of graduate school, a career and a shot at love, steered me aground. I'd felt held back a grade in adulthood after being rejected from UW. But now I held the power of the sea, propelling me forward. I would retake my GRE (Graduate Record Examination) test to improve my score and then reapply. I'd have to wait almost another year to hear whether or not I'd been accepted. In the meantime, I'd seek a job that paid chump change compared to the wages I could earn at sea. It was temporary until I could find a real job or another opportunity.

Though I focused on land, romantic images of Alaska resurfaced again and again, like a pod of orcas coming up for air. Memories of the difficult times had slowly drifted. The rise and fall of waves, ingrained in me, still rocked me to sleep each night as if I'd never left the ship. At times I'd suddenly wake, thinking I'd heard the sound of a haulback, only to find garbage trucks retrieving their catch in the alley between my apartment and the Thai restaurant. Seagulls called me on breezes through open windows. Sunrises and sunsets made me crave the sea like a lover. Post-Traumatic Sea Disorder. I couldn't let go of ocean life. My roots were trying to take hold on land, but the spinning compass at my core kept pulling me north toward Alaska.

19

∽∽∽

SINK OR SWIM

I'D been home from sea for two months when the doorbell rang. I was surprised to hear the familiar voice, deep and gentle, over the crackling intercom speaker.

"Hey Beautiful. I looked up your address in the phone book. I hope you don't mind me stopping by. I just got off the boat a few days ago. I have something for you."

I buzzed in Russell.

As I opened the door, the smell of *Obsession* filled my studio. My mind rushed back to the ship. Months had passed between us, and it was awkward to have my boat crush standing at my threshold. A near stranger to me now, I didn't know whether to high-five him or hug him.

"Come in. Welcome to my humble stateroom." I said, recalling the last time we were alone, bundled up in the storage locker on a windswept deck.

His stylish jeans and pressed shirt had replaced baggy sweats and orange raingear. His fade was freshly cut, and his beard was gone, revealing deep dimples. He looked older, more haggard than I'd remembered, but still handsome.

"Did you bring your anchor with you?" I asked.

"No, but I brought you these," he said. "Be careful. They're fragile."

I opened the box and unwrapped the tissue in my palm to reveal a calcified fan of snowflakes, a delicate coral. The other, the prized black coral, marbled gold, and coal twisted and branched like antlers the size of toothpicks. I pictured Russell getting off the ship, carrying a giant duffel bag in one hand and my boxed up precious treasures in the other.

"Thank you for the thoughtful gifts of nature. I love them. They're perfect."

"I knew you'd like them. You got really excited aboard ship whenever we'd hook something unusual." Sweet and kind; that was Russell.

He stumbled toward the window, prompting me to ask, "Why are you limping?"

"The boat took a roll and so did I. I would've fallen out the hatch if Dean wasn't there to grab me. I hope it heals fast so I can go back when the season reopens in January." It was August.

All the reasons to refrain from attaching to this fisherman—the dangers, the distance, the long periods of time spent apart, and limited communications—rushed into my mind.

Was a real relationship possible?

After months of freedom and unstructured living in Seattle, my strike-it-rich savings earned at sea were dwindling fast. I needed another job. My rent had increased another twenty-five bucks a month, a half-day's pay at a typical land job.

Following a thorough job hunt, the closest I came to stability was a seven-dollar-an-hour sales clerk position at an adventure clothing store. I became a khaki- and denim-clad clone—with frosty lipstick and colorful scarves mind you—greeting customers, straightening sleeves, and picking up piles of garments off dressing room floors. I wrapped shirts around a rectangular, plastic form and stacked the perfect folds into neat, easily toppled towers. Browsing shoppers would pull their selection from the middle of the stack in search of a medium, ignoring the little "M" stickers on the outside crease, where they could be easily seen. I straightened and folded over and over again, all day long. My work became a boring routine.

I was being sucked down a drain, swirling back into poverty. If I was to do a mundane job well, I at least needed to be compensated for it. I requested a meeting with the manager to pitch for a raise. I made the case I was a college-educated, outgoing, reliable hard worker with bills to pay. I needed more cashola to match my rent and cost-of-living increase.

She looked down at her acrylic, Vixen coral nails and said, "I'm sorry. I have to refuse your request for a raise and benefits."

"But I earned it." I listed the many reasons I deserved a pay increase while searching for some compassion, a heart that could be warmed to room temperature. I tried to bring her eyes up to meet mine. I thought maybe, like Captain Gus, she had the cursed black dot in the white of her eye leading to a dark tunnel.

"Why are you denying me a raise?" I questioned her.

"Why? Because you fail to cooperate with company policy."

It felt like someone had landed a right hook to my face. "*What* policy?" I wanted to say, "You mean the policy to fake smile, say "Hello," and act like we care about the customers when we're really just watching to see if they're shoplifting? Or is it the policy of making extra work for ourselves by constantly rearranging and moving the pants and shirts around, so it looks completely different every day when we return to the store and then can't find anything?"

She firmly pursed her lips and raised her eyebrows. "It's the socks," she said. "You're not selling the socks as asked." She flipped her blond bangs to reveal dark roots.

"You've *got* to be kidding?" I placed my hands on my temples, trying to ease the instant headache. "I'm not getting a raise, because I disagree with shoving eight-dollar socks down people's throats when they make a purchase to meet some sales quota? I have to work a full hour to buy a pair of socks from this place. My rent just went up twenty-five dollars a month. That's three pairs of socks. Half a day's salary."

I wanted to stand up and settle this injustice Bering Sea style: a gut punch or roundhouse kick sending her to the linoleum floor and letting her know how I really felt. If I had a camper, maybe I'd drive around the Seattle block and pull the poop-shoot like Mom. But I'd learned some control: don't blow a gasket, blow it off. I swallowed my frustration and contained any further comments before she outright fired me. It was the first job I ever hated, and I'd cleaned blood out from under a veterinarian's X-ray table with a toothbrush. I'd slipped back into a life funk. I wasn't seizing the day or seizing the pay, but couldn't quit this job until I found a different one.

I was also wrestling with the contrasts of love, lust, and ennui. Russell and I would see each other occasionally, but we were mismatched from the start. He was the summer crush on a camp counselor. He'd return to the *Nomad*; I'd press forward without him.

Luke, however, would always be magnetically imprinted on me, like a natal stream on a salmon smolt before it migrates out to sea and finds its way back home. With a continent between us, Luke and I continued to talk on the phone. I listened for cues to convince me to run to Florida and into a lifetime with him but remained on red flag alert.

Then I received a letter from Stef. She'd been in Alaska for just over two months on her second contract. Assigned to a shoreside catcher boat, she landed in and out of Dutch every three to four days. She'd already sent me a "home pack," a frozen case of squid and halibut that she'd caught recreationally in a skiff with her crew between fishing trips. Admittedly, I felt a bit envious. I wanted to turn and burn, to be shoreside with a new crew, too. I yearned for the sea, but I yearned even more for a career. On land. In her letter, Stef announced her engagement to *Muy Picante* Ben, her deckhand crush. What? Was she crazy? It was too soon. Her news killed my hope for our exotic trip together. Then I read, "Laura, I saw a dead body!"

At sea, we sometimes caught random items, such as bottles, boots, and gloves. And there were tales of hauling up bigger, grosser items like dead deer, whales, or other mammals. Stef's letter told the gruesome details of another boat that dumped their haul on deck to find what we, as observers and fishermen, collectively always dreaded—a dead human. She had gotten the gory details from the observer aboard, who had witnessed it all firsthand. I was reminded of Captain Gabe's story of gulls slurping eyeballs from floating carcasses eyeballs. This time, the fisherman's orange rain gear, customarily rubber-banded around the boots and sometimes the gloves, protected and held the corpse together. The only exposed part, the head, was missing. Like the sea lion that had been pulled up on her vessel, the man's head was devoured, likely by sand fleas. In port, she saw the body lowered into a metal casket and removed from the boat next to hers with a crane. This was something I hoped to never witness.

Despite Stef's tales of danger, difficult times, and a dead body, the magnetic buzz of Alaska was pulling me. Drudging through each day at the outfitter store, I folded shirt after shirt, and my natural smile was replaced by one from a plaster mold. I felt like a panhandler, "Hey, Consumer, want to throw down eight dollars and buy some extra socks you don't need so I can get a raise and some bennies?" I couldn't stand myself anymore—my life's purpose to sell, sell, sell to people who didn't need, need, need. I felt displaced and disconnected, and imagined myself far away, captured by a dimly lit horizon, circled by gulls, watching and waiting for an orca to breach.

One night at closing, a coworker and I finished "finessing" the shirts and jackets, meaning we pulled out every sleeve and fanned them in perfect order as if they were waving goodnight in unison. "Have a good weekend!" he said as we left.

Since I couldn't take time off from my sock-pushing, minimum-wage job I was celebrating Christmas in Seattle. Alone in my studio, I reminisced about Christmases past. Mom would have sped well over the speed limit and through red lights to get us, late, to Christmas Eve dinner at my Aunt Irene's house. By day, my aunt would have fully prepared a feast in her frilly apron, and by evening would've been tipping back her scotch and water over ice, saying in response to just about anything, "Well, la-dee-daa," and "Ahhh, hell, who cares." Irene's aunt, who we called Cha-Cha, a derivative of *ciotka*, which means aunt in Polish, would sit on the white couch covered in thick plastic, waving her cane and yelling absurdities. Two of my mom's three cousins would be laughing, loud and outrageous, like everything was an inside joke between them. The youngest cousin's long-term boyfriend, who was a little off-kilter, performed magic tricks like pulling a quarter from behind someone's ear or if you tapped his closed fist, into your palm popped red sponge creatures: a ball, a rabbit, or worse, a tiny foam penis with testicles. Something you don't want to see or have in your hand as a youth.

The night wouldn't be complete without Mom's tradition of dancing in a circle around Grandma in the center of the living room, while merrily singing, "Grandma got run over by a reindeer." The cousins would laugh, loud and sharp. My brother and

I, fingertips full of black olives, would laugh, too, but feeling sorry for Gram we'd say, "Mom, stop." Gram's boyfriend, who grew corn for Jiffy Pop and picked her up every Friday night for a date, would sit silently with his legs crossed, discreetly rolling his wolf blue eyes.

All night long my sweet brother would urge me to open only one present, his special gift to me, and then accidentally spill the beans on another's gift.

As happened one year, I'd opened his package and said, "Thanks Tom, I love this CD. But I don't have a CD player."

"Well, you will tomorrow," he replied, innocently spoiling the surprise.

Real, bold, friendly with strangers, and genuine to the core, no one had to guess who they were when no one was watching, or what they were thinking or feeling. Odd, zany, full of laughter, and possibly a few outbursts or brawls, they were the only family I had.

I'd retaken the GRE and improved my score dramatically. My application was off to the UW fisheries program for a second try. It was the end of year, a time of reflection when I asked, "Am I happy with what I've been doing for the past twelve months?" I was proud of my Bering Sea accomplishment; it kept my year from being a complete loss. But I had no clue what to do next. I'd been home for six months and applied for dozens of career-related jobs. But what environmental consultant or government agency would hire me now? I was a wannabe scientist working as a sock-pusher for minimum wage. On the verge of giving up, I sent out a spiritual Morse code to God: "SOS, Save Our Souls. Yo, God, I need a little help."

My answer came weeks later in January when I received an unexpected call. "Laura, we're in a bind." It was the fisheries observer contractor. "We desperately need trained observers to go to Dutch Harbor in three days. You'll receive three hundred dollars more per month than last time, and you can sign a two-month contract if you don't want to commit to three. However, we must have your answer by tomorrow."

"Tomorrow?" It was time to sink or swim. "OK. Let me sleep on it." I hung up and said aloud, "They need me."

Sleep on it? Who could sleep? I felt the same as that panicked night when I first moved to Seattle and wanted to run back to the familiar Ozarks. The decision was mine. This time I could leave a second-rate job on land and head back out to sea. Observer work required so much more of my mind and talents than a dead-end minimum-wage retail or waitress job. It was a job with a sense of urgency, a job not just anyone was qualified to do, one that gave me purpose and value. Above all, it was a break from having to make any decisions about my future. At sea, my life would hit pause and remove me from my land worries for a while.

This experience would be different from the first. It was the lucrative pollock-A season, where the pollock bellies are swollen full with jewels of roe. I'd be assigned to a 109-foot catcher boat. We'd trawl a midwater net for a relatively clean catch of pollock—the fish was typically turned into surimi (fake crab) or fish sticks—and then also fish P-cod. I knew P-cod well.

A smaller boat would have a small crew, probably less than six, and I bet they'd welcome my help in the galley and homemade cookies. Without processing capabilities, trips would last a few days at a time rather than a couple of months and spirits would be high. It was my chance for another fresh start. What did I have to lose except maybe my lunch over the icy railing of such a small vessel? Desperation pushed me, almost merrily, toward Dutch Harbor. Turn and burn! Bering Sea or bust!

The next morning, I marched into the clothing store with my head high and a proud chest, as if riding my horse Magic once again. I faced the manager with the dark roots and coral fingernails and said, "I'll work my shift today if you want me to, but otherwise, I quit. I'm going back to sea."

I meandered my way out through rounders of flannels and down jackets. I sang Johnny Paycheck's song, "Take this job [and those socks] and shove it." Doo-de-doo. "I ain't workin' here no more." My coworkers folded shirts with plastic boards and stacked them like toddlers with blocks. The overpriced socks hung by the register with eye-catching signage. I was done performing company tricks. My colleagues smiled goodbye with envy as I skipped out the exit for the last time. The appointed greeter for the day, my cool hiker friend, said, "Selling clothes fit for adventure isn't the same as living one. Have a nice weekend at sea." He winked.

Finally, I broke the news to my mom. "Mom, I just quit my retail job. I'm putting on my man boots and going back to Alaska."

"Oh no, I was afraid you'd do that."

She thought I'd gotten the risky part of my life out of my system. I thought I had, too. But once captured by the sea, it's hard to shake yourself free.

After a long goodbye, I hung up and realized Mom and my family struggles had helped shape me, and my security was no longer in Missouri, but rather aboard a fishing boat on Alaska's high seas. Like the bow of a ship I'd continue to rise up against each wave, each challenge as it hit me, fully aware of the calm to follow every storm.

Mom had told me many times before, "You're just stronger than me and your brother." If I was, I hadn't known it. When I was younger, I always looked up to Mom. She was the strong one to me, married and divorced young, raising two kids alone on a bartender's salary, refusing to go on welfare. She raised a son with an undiagnosed disability, got us through my tragic go-kart accident and the death of our young father. My brother went through life not understanding the complexities around him, but still he pushed on and rarely complained. To me, that was true strength.

Now I would aim for that place on the horizon between earth and sky, between where I came from and where I was headed. And though there was no safe place on a fishing vessel on the Bering Sea, it is where I found solid ground, my shelter, and my strength, doing what I was now well-trained to do. The possibilities of my future, of success, now outweighed my fear of failure.

Others had believed in me, but it took a journey out west and three challenging months on the Bering Sea to prove I was more capable, resilient, and self-reliant—stronger—than I knew. I would leave on this next adventure for me, for Mom, for my brother, and for all those who struggle to push beyond their limits in search of a better life. Now it was time to ship out again—for round two of the beauty, and the brutality, of the Bering Sea.

EPILOGUE

LOOKING back now, decades later, it's clear I didn't understand then how moving to Seattle and choosing the turbulent Bering Sea would impact me in the long term. I thought my first fisheries observer contract would have been my last, and I thought the same with the second, that is, until I jumped aboard my third vessel. Each contract uncovered a new variety of fish, fishing methods and gear, fishermen crushes, and a more intimate view of Dutch Harbor. I lived those two years in a whirlwind, hopping the stepping stones of three- to four-month-long contracts at sea, still hoping to find meaningful work on land and acceptance into grad school.

I couldn't have anticipated what came next. Sadly, I would be rejected from UW a second time, but an acceptance letter from Humboldt State stopped the bleeding, at least for a while. I basked in my own glow for weeks until I met with the professor on campus. To my surprise, my research species would be switched from the thirty-pound California halibut to teensy *tubesnouts*. Worse, and this was *worse*—my research funding was yanked. I'd have to pay the high out-of-state tuition and probably wait tables again to make it. I saw my two years of hard-earned Bering Sea ka-ching go ker-plunk. The news shot holes into my dream, sending it sinking to the bottom of the ocean. Fast. Like a 700-pound crab pot.

Resolution came somewhere between me sobbing and slumped over a plate of petrale sole with lemon wedges and the ten-hour drive back to Seattle. The road to graduate school had been long, and it wasn't supposed to play out this way. The opportunity didn't match my gut, my internal compass, and the only direction I would need to follow. I'd been schooled by University Bering Sea and Professor Stormy Weather. Without a tuition scholarship, Humboldt, or any other program, was not for me. I was stronger now, strong enough to listen to my heart and walk away.

Now, decades later, I stand on a cobble beach, at the confluence of a salmon stream and Puget Sound, in the shadow of Mount Rainier, my anchor to the Pacific Northwest. The brackish waters lap and swirl around my XtraTufs, the sound a familiar pulse, like my own heartbeat. These waters, linked to the Bering Sea by the Pacific Ocean, have pushed and pulled and shaped and held me close. I'm taken back to the day I moved to Seattle, questioning my decision but bursting with hope and determination. I couldn't have known I made the right choice until I could look back at the hills I've climbed. I wouldn't have known I would live with arms wide open to adventures like sailing, skydiving, backpacking, and snowshoeing in the mountains, and traveling internationally, often solo.

I didn't know then I'd still be in touch with Luke after all these years, who occasionally calls when he "needs a moral compass," the ear and genuine love of a trustworthy friend, or someone who'll answer, "Let-me-think-about-it-yes" to a spontaneous offer to seek that which lies out of reach for most others.

I also couldn't have known that the Alaska cruise I took my dad Walter on would be our last before he perished quickly from lung cancer.

I wouldn't have guessed the observer manual, in which I'd inscribed "WORRY MORE!" would nearly double in size, from 327 pages in my Bering Sea days to 589 at last count.

And I never would have guessed I'd write and publish this book.

In my Bering Sea days, I didn't think I could consider myself successful or happy if one of the links in my plan were broken. I thought I had only one chance to get life right, but quickly discovered if I ventured down one path and it didn't work out, I could choose another. Life's value wasn't in getting the guy, or the job, or acceptance into a program. Sometimes our dreams are slow to be fulfilled, and sometimes they never are, but with effort and an open heart full of hope, those derailed dreams are replaced by other equally satisfying dreams.

Standing along the Puget Sound shoreline today, I feel one boot rooting into the earth and other loosening, drawing me toward the sea. I scan back on my journey. My simplistic ambition was to be wedged between the mountains and the ocean and to become some kind of an -ist. Serving as a wetland and stream ecologist for more than twenty years, I reflect back on that long-ago fairytale goal, and I am ecstatic, for that's exactly where I am. I couldn't have predicted that either.

Not a week goes by that I don't think of my time at sea, forever etched in my soul. I've encountered some of the most incredible men (and a few women) with the most dangerous jobs in the world. For a time, I became part of a tight subculture, a society that I never would have understood had I not lived it. I will never again in the same way view any oceangoing vessel, or order *fish and chips* from a menu, or pass through a fresh seafood market, or don boots and rain gear. On the streets of Seattle, I easily spot the commercial fishermen fresh off the ships like those I lived with side by side at sea. They're unshaven, bushy haired, wearing sweatpants or dirty work jeans and hooded sweatshirts, and probably holding a cigarette in their rough-skinned hands. Jackets embroidered with their ships, their tribes, cover their labored backs. They still feel the surge of sea beneath their XtraTufs planted firmly on the ground, but especially when they lay down and close their eyes at night. They're grateful to be home, to be alive, and to have money in their pockets. Immersed in their at-sea world, I became stronger because of my work alongside them. Now, during the difficult times, when I think for a moment *I can't*, I press through until I remember, *I can*. These fishermen, like me, have powered through many Bering Sea struggles. They're Bering Sea strong . . . and so am I.

ACKNOWLEDGMENTS

THIS book first began as a typed copy of my personal journal entries with the hope that pieces of life seen through my eyes would someday hold meaning to someone besides myself. The more I filled in the voids, the more I wanted to share my stories to entertain and encourage. I'm grateful to God for placing many angels in my assorted paths as I wrote this book. Many go unnamed, but to a few I am indebted and must thank them here.

There is a saying, "He is my backbone," to represent a friend who is more like family. Stephanie Teal—my best friend, who I met in the parking lot on day one of this Alaskan journey—is my backbone and my greatest gift. Who knew our Alaskan adventure would lead to a lifetime of friendship that would outlast any hardship to come our way? Thanks, my soul sister, for your constant support, humor, and voice of reason in my life.

Leslie Leyland Fields, author, speaker, and Alaskan fisherwoman, you have held up me, my writing journey, and these chapters like bookends. You've taught, guided, mentored, and advised me on all levels from faith to writing to life. I am grateful for your talents and your friendship.

Theo Nestor, author and teacher, you coached me in my first draft and encouraged me in my struggle near the end. I hope your efforts find some reward in these pages.

Chuck Thompson, your writing has both left me on edge and laughing out loud in public, causing people to stare at me. I owe you special thanks, as I'm convinced your work serendipitously led me to this book's publication. You graciously answered my beg-o-grams with heaps of advice when I needed it most. You are a dang funny gem of a man.

Daryl Grigsby, my friend, I thank you for making me stand on a Seattle street corner and shout, "I am a writer!" In the periods of doubt, which were many, I echoed your words, "Hartema, just write the damn story and have fun with it." Thanks for your early support in this endeavor.

In addition to those mentioned above, I send a thanks to the following for your graciousness, who helped without pausing: Suzan Chiacchio Brand, Heather MacLaren Johnson, Laura Peterson, Anne Biklé, Amanda Hubbard, Wendy Gable Collins, Mark Leary, and Jonathan Allen.

To my agent, Joelle Delbourgo; my editor, Brooke Rockwell; and Skyhorse Publishing—thanks to you for taking a chance on this first-time author, believing in my story, and shepherding me through to the end.

My final thanks and admiration is to all the rough-and-tumble commercial fishermen in the world for their hard work. To the men who blessed and cursed me aboard ship, you made this sea story worth telling. *Bering Sea Strong*, baby!